BENEFITS OF PLANNING & BOOKING AT INSIGHTGUIDES.COM/HOLIDAYS

PLANNED BY LOCAL EXPERTS

The Insight Guides local experts are hand-picked, based on their experience in the travel industry and their impeccable standards of customer service.

SAVE TIME & MONEY

When a local expert plans your trip, you save time and money when you book, even during high season. You won't be charged for using a credit card either.

TAILOR-MADE TRIPS

Book with Insight Guides, and you will be in complete control of the planning process, from the initial selections to amending your final itinerary.

BOOK & TRAVEL STRESS-FREE

Enjoy stress-free travel when you use the Insight Guides secure online booking platform. All bookings come with a money-back guarantee.

WHAT OTHER TRAVELLERS THINK ABOUT TRIPS BOOKED AT INSIGHTGUIDES.COM/HOLIDAYS

Trip to Vietnam

The organization was superb, the drivers professional, and accommodation quite comfortable. I was well taken care of! My thanks to your colleagues who helped make my trip to Vietnam such a great experience. My only regret is that I couldn't spend more time in the country.

Heather ★★★★★

TOP 10 ATTRACTIONS

CATHEDRAL OF ST JOHN THE DIVINE
The Cathedral contains beautiful stained-glass windows, including one depicting the crucifixion. See page 26.

REDCLIFFE QUAY
Shops and stalls jostle for space along the waterfront, one of the oldest parts of St John's. See page 33.

GREAT BIRD ISLAND
Boat parties come here to birdwatch, picnic on the pristine beach, and for some of the best snorkelling in Antigua. See page 46.

HALF MOON BAY
This crescent-shaped sheltered bay is considered one of the best in the world. See page 54.

BETTY'S HOPE
Antigua's first sugar plantation is a valuable heritage site. See page 48.

DEVIL'S BRIDGE
Waves crash against the rocks and water shoots through a blowhole at this natural landmark. See page 51.

NELSON'S DOCKYARD
At English Harbour, this splendidly restored Georgian naval base is now also a renowned yachting centre. See page 58.

SHIRLEY HEIGHTS
Save Sunday for a trip to the Heights when it's packed with visitors and Antiguans enjoying steel pan and reggae music, and brilliant views. See page 63.

FIG TREE DRIVE
A drive inland reveals lush tropical vegetation and fragrant fruit trees, and the chance to fly through the trees on a zip line. See page 76.

BARBUDA
Taking the catamaran to Barbuda for the day should include a visit to the impressive Frigate Bird Sanctuary. See page 77.

A PERFECT DAY

7.00am

Dickenson Bay

The days start early on Antigua. Head to Dickenson Bay and take a leisurely stroll along this long stretch of beach while losing yourself in the early morning solitude. Sit back, relax and enjoy a stress-free breakfast at the Bay House Restaurant (Trade Winds Hotel) looking out over the Caribbean Sea.

11.00am

South coast

Travel to the south coast for a visit to Nelson's Dockyard, passing through All Saints, the second largest town on Antigua. En route to the Dockyard, stop off at Falmouth Harbour and take a wander down the jetty to gaze in amazement at the floating gin palaces tied up here.

12 noon

Nelson's Dockyard

At English Harbour, Nelson's Dockyard is the only existing Georgian dockyard in the world and is now a designated National Park. There are many restored sites to visit within the parameters, plus an interesting museum.

9.00am

St John's

Check out St John's, where shopping opportunities abound on the waterfront at Heritage and Redcliffe quays, a picturesque area of preserved buildings. Pause for a coffee break at Harbour View in Redcliffe Quay, known as a great people-watching spot.

1.30pm

Shirley Heights

Ascend the hill for lunch at Shirley Heights Lookout and be rewarded with terrific views out over English Harbour and beyond.

ON **ANTIGUA**

3.00pm

Beach time

Head west along the coast passing many sensational beaches. Divert off at Ffryes Bay to spend time relaxing on the sand soaking up the sun's rays or taking a dip in the warm sea. Sun loungers and snorkelling gear are available to rent (there is a reef right off the shore where you can check out the sea life).

5.00pm

Sunset

The west coast is the perfect spot from which to be captivated by the sun setting over the Caribbean Sea. So hang around a bit longer at Dennis's Cocktail Bar (Happy Hour 4–6pm), sip a tropical cocktail and be awestruck by the magical sunset.

6.30pm

Nightlife

If you want to freshen up, return to your accommodation before heading out to Dickenson Bay for dinner at Coconut Grove open-air restaurant. After dinner, hang out, chill and party at BeachLimerz on Fort James Beach.

2.30pm

Rainforest drive

Head back to All Saints and take a scenic spin down Fig Tree Drive, which twists and turns its way through the lush rainforest back towards the coast; a great way to see the island's tropical foliage and pick up some local crafts at Fig Tree Studio Art Gallery. If you want to see more, book to come back another day and take the zip line adventure suspended above the rainforest.

CONTENTS

INTRODUCTION

The sister islands of Antigua and Barbuda may be justly celebrated for their endless strips of gleaming white and pink-sand bays, warm turquoise waters and the welcoming smiles and laughter of the locals, but this is just where it begins.

Diving enthusiasts will delight in the unrivalled coral reefs, while yachtsmen gather from around the world during the sailing season, and sunbathers and ornithologists have equal reasons to step ashore and follow their passions.

Beyond the beach, there are interesting historical sites reflecting the nation's past, such as Nelson's Dockyard and the sugar plantation Betty's Hope. Antigua houses the nation's bustling capital, St John's, a captivating glimpse of the urban Caribbean. Here the jumble of traditional clapboard houses stand side by side with modernity, while brightly painted warehouses have been converted into shops and restaurants, and fishing boats bob alongside cruise ships in the harbour.

The gently undulating wooded hills of southwest Antigua reveal exotic vegetation and stand out in a landscape otherwise scoured for sugar plantations. The island of Barbuda offers quite different vistas and is an eco-lover's paradise, secluded and untouched.

All that said, the only way to truly appreciate Antigua and Barbuda, in the memorable words of the islander's, is 'lime man' (hang out, chill out and party).

GEOGRAPHY AND CLIMATE

The largest of the Leeward Islands (108sq miles/280sq km), Antigua lies on the northeast shoulder of the Caribbean archipelago, 450 miles (725km) east of Hispaniola. On clear days you can see Montserrat's volcano smoking to the southwest,

while Guadeloupe's shores are visible on the southerly horizon. Antigua and Barbuda was once one sedimentary land mass, scythed apart 12,000 years ago when sea levels rose and flooded the lands.

The islands are among the driest in the region, which ensures that visitors can bask in warm, sunny weather whenever they go, while trade winds help to keep you cool. Hurricanes are rare on these islands but early warning systems help the region to weather the storms.

Male frigatebird

THE ENVIRONMENT

Given the lowest rainfall levels in the Caribbean, Antiguan and Barbudan landscapes lack the tropical lushness associated with neighbouring islands. The plantations carved away the woods and this cut in the hydrological cycle is blamed by many for the limited rainfall today. There are no rivers, heightening the value of water – hotels often advise visitors to temper any unnecessary water usage. However, the higher parts of the island in the more richly vegetated hills of the southwest can offer a rainforest effect when after occasional downpours, water gushes down the hillsides, providing temporary glimpses of what might have been. Fig Tree Drive remains a celebrated route of wild bananas, lianas and would-be rainforest.

Basket weavers ply their trade on the beaches

FLORA AND FAUNA

Over 150 varieties of birds can be found on the islands. The yellow-breasted bananaquit, known as the sugar bird, one of the most common, can be seen darting around brilliantly coloured blossoms. Tiny, brightly hued humming-birds abound, hovering amid flowering bushes. The offshore islands and man-grove lagoons that fringe parts of the coastline are home to herons and lum-bering pelicans.

Barbuda has many species of bird, listing brown boobies, pelicans, herons, laughing gulls, terns and white-crowned pigeons. Black-necked stilts, bridled quail doves and West Indian tree ducks vie for air space with white-cheeked ducks and marbled godwits. The mangrove swamp in Codrington Lagoon was home to a nesting colony of over 5,000 frigate birds but the colony diminished following hurricane Irma in 2017. However, the numbers are steadily increasing again.

Antigua plays host to a number of rare or endangered crea-tures. Hawksbill turtles nest on Long Island, and the Hawksbill Sea Turtle Research Project has been undertaking crucial studies of the species since the mid-1980s. The Antigua racer snake is among the rarest in the world, with a colony of only a hundred or so inhabiting Great Bird Island. Since the 17th century, when Barbuda was leased to the Codringtons to raise

livestock to feed Antigua, the descendants of the first goats and deer have roamed through the logwood and lignum vitae of the bush, surviving several centuries of human settlement.

IDENTITY AND POPULATION

Politically there are dissimilarities between Antigua and Barbuda. The two islands are uneasy political associates, as the distinctive cultural pride of Barbudans fiercely underpins calls for greater autonomy from the bigger sister island. Yet there is more that unites than divides them.

The population of Antigua and Barbuda is around 94,000 – a kaleidoscope of peoples from other Caribbean islands, as well as all over the world – with most residing in St John's parish and the rest scattered throughout the islands. Barbuda's residents mostly share the main settlement of Codrington.

Antiguans and Barbudans are some of the friendliest people in the world. An atmosphere of warmth and good humour prevails,

⊙ TIE THE KNOT

Antigua and Barbuda, known as the 'Romance Capital of the Caribbean', is very popular for getting married. All the ingredients for romance are here: white beaches perfect for moonlit strolls, swaying palm trees and glowing sunsets. Getting married is a breeze on these islands; exchange your vows on a beautiful palm-fringed beach, or get married in a church provided you allow additional time to fulfil church formalities. Some UK travel agents arrange holidays that include the costs of the wedding. Many hotels have their own wedding gazebos where marriages take place, and wedding planners are on hand to assist. The administrative details are minor (see page 133).

Galley Bay

as well as a 'no problem' attitude towards life.

TOURISM AND THE ECONOMY

As the Antiguan sugar industry waned from the late 19th century the economy began to falter, revived by US military investment during the 1940s and 1950s, when an infrastructure was put into place to develop a new economic presence: upmarket tourism.

These days the economy is driven primarily by tourism. Around 63 percent of the working population are employed in a tourist industry, which provides 69 percent of the national income. The benefits have largely outweighed the costs; new forms of more sensitive tourism have been pioneered, and the range of activities and events in which tourists may engage has been extended to the benefit of islanders and visitors alike. But tourism does have its drawbacks. Some of the most stunning beaches are no longer deserted as luxury resorts have emerged as a backdrop.

Despite the force of hurricane Irma in 2017, Antigua has been relatively unaffected. In fact, the island welcomed a record-breaking number of visitors in 2018, which is predicted to continue climbing. Sadly, it is a different story for Barbuda having been completely devastated by the hurricane. But the future is looking brighter as Barbuda rebuilds and slowly finds its place in the tourism market once again.

A BRIEF HISTORY

The first human traces on Antigua are believed to date back to the Stone Age Siboney people who migrated from South America to settle on the island around 2400 BC. They were followed by the seafaring Arawak-speaking farmers and fishermen around the first century AD, who settled in villages around the coast and also developed their skill in pottery making.

EARLY TIMES

The Arawaks were the first well-documented group of Antiguans. They were a peaceful people, catching fish and growing corn and cassava, and soon introduced an agricultural system into the islands of Antigua and Barbuda. Crops were developed including sweet potatoes, chillies, guava, tobacco, cotton and the famous 'black' pineapple. Their tribes were ruled by a chief or cacique and their religious leader or shaman was held in great respect. From around AD 600 they suffered continuous raids from another tribe, the Caribs, a more warlike race from the Amazon region with superior weaponry and seafaring prowess.

By AD 1100 the Caribs had finally conquered all the Arawak lands and reigned supreme over the Leeward Islands. They did not, however, settle on the island of Antigua but used it as a base for gathering provisions.

EUROPEAN COLONISATION

In 1493, on his second voyage, Christopher Columbus sighted the island of Antigua and named it Santa Maria de la Antigua, after the miracle-working saint of Seville in Spain. Early settlement, however, was discouraged by insufficient water on the island and by Carib raids. Columbus was followed by the English, French

Slaves planting sugar cane, Antigua (1823 illustration)

and Dutch, all of whom fought for dominion over the islands. In 1632 Antigua was colonised by a British expedition from St Kitts, under Sir Thomas Warner and the first settlement was established at Parham, which became the home of the early British governors. Antigua remained under the rule of the English with only a brief takeover by the French in 1666.

Once returned to the crown, with the Peace of Breda in 1667, the island became an important colonial naval base, with an arsenal built at English Harbour in the south of the island where the British fleet was stationed. Sugar was introduced in the 1650s and in 1674 Christopher Codrington established the first sugar estate at Betty's Hope, which remained in the family for almost 200 years. In 1680 he leased the island of Barbuda, where he raised livestock and grew agricultural produce with slave labour for the British colonists on Antigua. Codrington and his contemporaries brought slaves from Africa's west coast to work the plantations under brutal conditions. Meanwhile Antigua was deforested to make way for the plantations, which were devoted solely to the production of sugar. The number of slaves on Antigua peaked at 37,500 in the 1770s, but thousands more died during the crossing.

In 1784 Horatio Nelson arrived as captain of the HMS *Boreas*, which was based in English Harbour – Antigua was used as the

headquarters of the British Royal Navy Caribbean fleet. The harbour provided a sheltered and well-protected deep water port. Known as the 'gateway to the Caribbean' the formidable base ensured Britain's enemies gave the whole island a wide berth. Nelson's time as commander of the fleet between 1784 and 1787 is commemorated at Nelson's Dockyard. Nelson spent almost all of his time in the cramped quarters of his ship as he had a distinct dislike of the island calling it a 'dreadful hole'.

In 1807 the slave trade was finally abolished but slavery on the plantations continued. With all the others in the British Empire, Antiguan slaves were emancipated in 1834 and some 29,000 slaves were freed. Many, however, remained economically dependent on their plantation owners. In fact, fair rights for workers remained a problem until the 1940s. Further problems occurred on Antigua during the 1830s and 1840s when the island was hit by earthquakes, hurricanes, drought and yellow fever. To compound all this, a fire destroyed most of the capital, St John's. By the 1850s the sugar industry was in crisis with further hurricanes and drought, together with reduced commodity prices. The industry continued to wane and in just a century no more sugar was produced in Antigua, the last plantation closing in 1971.

Until the development of tourism in the past few decades, Antiguans struggled for prosperity, eking out a poor agricultural existence and in 1938 the Moyne Commission for the West

Decadent landowners

On the same island, but worlds apart, life for the white-planter classes suffered more from decadence than want. John Luffman writes in A Brief Account of the Island of Antigua (1789) that 'men sport several dishes at their tables, drink claret, keep mulato mistresses, and indulge in every foolish extravagance'.

Indies recorded Antigua among the most impoverished of the islands. Poor labour conditions persisted until 1939 when a member of a royal commission urged the formation of a trade union movement. A short-term boost came to the economy during World War II when the US built two military bases, creating some local employment.

POLITICAL DEVELOPMENT

The Antigua Trades and Labour Union (ATLU), formed in 1939, was a direct response to the miserable working conditions. It was created under the leadership of Vere Cornwall Bird (1910–1999) who had been an officer in the Salvation Army for two years, while pursuing his interests in trade unionism and politics. On seeing how the landowners were treating the local black Antiguans and Barbudans, he decided to leave the Salvation Army to follow a political career.

⊘ CONTINUING ENSLAVEMENT

The voice of the enslaved is poignantly recounted in *The History of Mary Prince, a West Indian Slave, Related by Herself*. This narrative bears witness to the ills of the age as experienced by a woman in St John's during the early 18th century. Emancipation came in 1834, but not before a series of slave rebellions had ensured that the days of the regime were numbered. The most famous revolt occurred in 1736 and, if successful, would have altered the course of Caribbean history. Given the sugar monopoly, former slaves, once freed, had little choice of alternative work, and most remained on the plantations. For the planters, the cost of wage labour turned out to be lower than the upkeep of the slave system.

Under Bird's strong leadership the labour movement – now the Antigua Labour Party (ALP) – gained momentum culminating in his victory at the first ever local elections in 1946, winning a seat in the legislature and appointed a member of the Executive Council. An imposing figure – he stood at 7ft (213cm) – he was a brilliant orator, wowed the masses and became the dominant political and economic force on the island.

Vere Cornwall Bird, first Prime Minister of Antigua and Barbuda

He led the Antiguan people into the post-colonial era with rousing rhetoric but made it clear in the 1950s and 1960s that the island still operated as two separate societies, the whites and 'the rest'.

Antigua, together with Barbuda and Redonda as dependencies, became the first East Caribbean island to be appointed an Associated State of the Commonwealth in 1967. The national flag comprising the sun rising on a black background with bands of blue, then white, narrowing to a 'V' for victory, bordered by red, was elaborately designed for this occasion. The sun depicts the dawn of a new era; red, symbolises the people's dynamism; black belongs to the island's soil and African heritage; while gold, white and blue signal the soul of tourist heritage – the sun, sand and sea.

Bird, radical in his younger days, had been shifting to the right, and in the face of severe social unrest that forced a split in the ALP in 1967 and rioting in 1968, the ALP lost its tight hold of Antigua

The Brute Force Steel Band of Antigua in 1965

and Barbuda politics. Out of the split, the Antigua Workers Union was formed and later the Progressive Labour Movement. In 1971 the so-called 'Broom Election' swept the Progressive Labour Movement and George Walter to victory, clearing out the Bird administration. But just five years later, in 1981, a 95 percent turnout returned V. C. Bird or 'Papa' Bird as he was known, as premier, and Antigua and Barbuda to independence. Queen Elizabeth II remains the Head of State for this constitutional monarchy to this day, and is represented by a Governor General. In June 1981 Antigua and Barbuda joined the Organisation of Eastern Caribbean States (OECS), which promotes economic co-operation, trade and joint action on major common problems. Since the 1960s the two islands have gradually abandoned their agricultural economy and turned their sights on becoming a tourist paradise.

In 1989 The Barbuda People's Movement gained all nine seats on the Barbuda Council and campaigned vociferously for greater autonomy. It did not, however, gain enough votes to qualify for a seat in the national government.

INDEPENDENT NATION

In 1992 the three opposition parties merged to form the United Progressive Party in an attempt to overthrow the Bird dynasty and

the Antigua Labour Party. V.C. Bird, however, led the new state until 1994, when his son Lester B. Bird took over the reins. As times changed, the lines of power and money became more interwoven within the Bird clan and their networks of associates. Flows of large investments from abroad, without signs of obvious gain for the people of Antigua, and an embarrassing series of offshore financial scandals, lowered the tone of government business.

The colonial schemes of the past are more than matched by today's intriguing political scene, which has thrown up corruption and money laundering matters by the bucketful. The Bird family, masterminded by the late V.C. Bird, held a stern grip on the country's political, economic and media matters for over five decades. In 1997 a series of financial scandals and the collapse of a major Antiguan bank provoked international condemnation

⊙ HISTORY OF REDONDA

The uninhabited island of Redonda became part of Antigua and Barbuda in 1967, despite it lying some 35 miles (56km) southwest of Antigua. Home to a large number of seabirds, the resultant deposit of guano became a viable commercial product in the mid-19th century before the advent of artificial fertilisers. From the 1860s until World War I a few hardy souls – a population of 120 were living there in 1901 – made a good living collecting and shipping bird droppings to Britain.

Despite being annexed by the British, Matthew Shiell, an Irishman from Montserrat, allegedly claimed the island as a kingdom in 1865, crowning his son, an author, the first king. The title has since passed to a succession of non-resident literary types who have created honorary peers including poet Dylan Thomas, actor Vincent Price and musician Sting.

Sir Rodney Williams, 4th Governor General of Antigua and Barbuda, meeting Queen Elizabeth

of the islands' financial sector. In 2004 the United Progressive Party, led by Baldwin Spencer won the general election defeating the Antigua Labour Party and ending Lester B. Bird's 10-year reign.

Tourism increased its monopoly of the economy. With huge investment from the US and more recently China, luxury resorts attracted more and more visitors. However, fraud and financial scandal were still rife. In 2009 Sir Allen Stanford, a financier and businessman was arrested by the FBI for fraud, receiving a 110-year prison sentence. As Antigua's second largest employer after the government, his demise resulted in massive job losses.

Power was returned to the Antigua Labour Party under the leadership of Gaston Browne in the election of 2014 and again in 2018. Controversy has plagued Browne's career with his involvement with overseas investment for mega-resort developments, allegations of corruption and in his complex relationship with Barbuda. The Land Act of 2007 upheld that all land in Barbuda was held freely and in common and Barbudans had a right to self-determination and to develop their land for sustainable, small-scale tourism. Under Gaston Browne the Land Act was repealed in 2015, and since Hurricane Irma in 2017 the situation has been exacerbated, resulting in a legal battle for the rights of the Barbudan people who are anxious to retain their individuality.

HISTORICAL LANDMARKS

c.2400 BC Nomadic Siboney 'stone people' populate the island.

1st century AD The Arawak people establish agriculture and trade.

1100 The Caribs conquer Arawak lands.

1493 Columbus names the island – Santa María de la Antigua.

1525 Spanish settlers land, but Caribs force them out.

1632 The island is colonised by the British.

1674 Christopher Codrington establishes the first sugar estate.

1784–87 Horatio Nelson arrives as commander of the fleet.

1807 The slave trade is abolished but slavery persists.

1830s–40s Antigua is hit by several natural disasters.

1834 Slavery is finally abolished.

1850s Sugar industry in crisis.

1938 Antigua among the most impoverished of the West Indies.

1941 Military bases extend US influence in the region.

1946 The Antigua Labour Party (ALP) wins local elections, led by V.C. Bird.

1967 The islands become an Associated State of the Commonwealth.

1968 Antigua becomes a popular port of call for large cruise ships.

1971 The last sugar plantation ceases production.

1981 'Papa' Bird leads the islands to full independence.

1989 Barbuda People's Movement campaigns for greater autonomy.

1993 V.C. Bird retires from politics; his son Lester B. Bird succeeds him.

1995 Hurricane Luís causes $300-million of damage.

2002 Tourism generates about 60 percent of the island's income.

2004 The United Progressive Party wins the general election.

2009 Sir Allen Stanford arrested for fraud, causing massive job losses.

2014 The ALP, led by Gaston Browne, wins 12 June election.

2017 Hurricane Irma hits the islands. Antigua escapes serious damage but Barbuda is devastated and the island is evacuated.

2018 Gaston Browne and the ALP retain power at the election in March.

2019 Barbuda is open again for tourists, but its future autonomy is in conflict with the Antiguan government.

View over English Harbour from Shirley Heights

WHERE TO GO

Antigua's scalloped, irregular coastline is one of its chief delights, so it is no surprise that most of the action takes place on or near the water. Fine natural harbours have welcomed sailors to the island for generations, and sailing is big news.

History buffs should make for Nelson's Dockyard, the world's only working Georgian dockyard, and visit Shirley Heights to enjoy panoramic views. St John's is well worth a visit for its colourful waterfront and fine cathedral, while the stunning inland scenery of the rainforest is matched by coastal wonders such as Devil's Bridge. Just a short ferry ride from Antigua, Barbuda bakes quietly in the sun. Top attractions here are the mind-blowing, pinkish sand beaches, and ornithologists will delight at the frigate bird nesting grounds.

The best way to explore is by taking one of the many organised tours, or by taxi on a 'round the island' tour escorted by a local, very informative fun driver.

ST JOHN'S

Charmingly time-worn, **St John's ❶** is an appealing West Indian town sloping gently back from the waterfront. A melting pot of candy-coloured architecture lines the orderly pattern of streets and narrow alleys. Clapboard buildings with fretwork balconies cluster on the hill below the cathedral, which is the best place to start exploring – unless, of course, you are coming straight off a cruise ship docked in the quay.

CATHEDRAL OF ST JOHN THE DIVINE

The skyline of St John's is dominated by the 70ft (21 metres) twin towers of the **Cathedral of St John the Divine** Ⓐ. The great parish church, with its walled, shady churchyard, covers a wide block between Newgate and Long streets. The towers, topped with shiny grey cupolas, are impressive, especially for those arriving by sea, and have earned St John's the reputation as 'the most imposing of all the cathedrals in the West Indies'.

It is also called 'a church within a church', because after the first wooden structure built on this site in 1683–84 was destroyed by fire, and a second stone building severely damaged by the great earthquake in 1834, it was decided that radical measures were needed. Consequently, the present building, completed in 1847 and consecrated on 25 July the following year, was given

St John's waterfront

a pitch pine interior and a stone exterior, as a defence against both fire and earthquake. Subsequent minor tremors and the earthquake of 1974 have taken their toll, however. A great deal of renovation was completed in time for the 150th anniversary in 1998, but improvement works are still ongoing.

The iron gates on the south face of the church are flanked by pillars displaying lead figures of St John the Divine and St John the Baptist. They were taken by HMS *Temple* in 1756, from a French ship destined for neighbouring Martinique, during the Seven Years' War between England and France. The cathedral can be entered through these gates, through those on Newgate Street, or via small gates on either side.

The cruciform interior of the church includes an octagonal high altar, made of mahogany, which was presented in 1926 in memory of Robert McDonald, a former chancellor of the diocese. The beautiful stained-glass windows that allow light to flood over the altar portray the Crucifixion of the Lord with the Virgin Mary and St John the Divine. The Blessed Sacrament Chapel is located to the left of the high altar and the War Memorial Chapel is on the right. The inside was opened again in 2018 following restoration, which is ongoing.

AROUND INDEPENDENCE AVENUE

Nearby, east of the cathedral off Independence Avenue, is **Government House**, the office of the Governor General, the British Crown's representative on the island. Originally called Parsonage House, due to its proximity to the cathedral, it was owned by a wealthy local man, Thomas Nasbury Kerby. When a suitable official residence was sought for the new governor, Lord Lavington, in 1800, the house was rented by the government because it was 'detached and pretty'. The following year it was acquired as a permanent home for the island's governors and additions were made

to enlarge and embellish it. The house was extended again in 1860 in preparation for a royal visit by Prince Alfred, who was travelling on HMS *St George*. Government House fell into disrepair over the years, until major renovations were begun in 1996.

The **Cenotaph** stands at the top of High Street, which runs into Independence Avenue. It is a monument to the Antiguans who died in World War I, and was unveiled in August 1919, almost a year after the war ended. Special services are held here each Remembrance Day to honour those who lost their lives during both the 20th-century world wars.

The **Antigua Recreation Ground ⑧** on Factory Road, known locally simply as 'ARG', was once the prime stadium for all beloved Test matches. Now not much more than a shrine to West Indian Cricketer and local hero Sir Vivian Richards, record breaking moments have enshrined the ARG in Antiguan history. You can still see the roll of honour boards that proudly display who scored a 100 or more runs and those who took five wickets or more in a match. Today, the run-down venue may have been over-shadowed by the new Sir Vivian Richards Stadium (see page 87), but to the elation of Antiguans, the occasional event is still held at the ARG, helped along by joyous music and entertainment. The annual

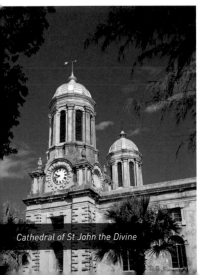
Cathedral of St John the Divine

Inside Government House

Carnival celebrations are centred on the Recreation Ground and it is also used for big parades, including the Independence Day Parade on 1 November, celebrating Antigua's independence.

On the other side of Factory Road is the Rappaport Centre, an angular white building set in landscaped grounds that houses the National Archives. The centre borders the **Botanical Gardens** Ⓒ, established in 1893 with the aim of providing a green and open space in the bustling capital and promoting an awareness of the natural environment.

At one time the gardens, which span several acres, were a popular spot but in the 1950s they deteriorated and for some time they were rarely used. Some restoration work was carried out in 1987 by the Botanical Gardens Society, but the society itself declined over the years, and two major hurricanes took their toll on the grounds during the 1990s. Today, the gardens, while partially restored, remain rather neglected.

Despite their slightly lacklustre state, the grounds can provide a wonderful shady spot in which to cool off in the middle of a hot day's sightseeing or shopping, and there are still some plants worthy of note if you care to explore – look for the majestic zulu tree (*Ficus nekbuda*), which is nearly 90 years old. There are also specimens of Cuban royal palm (*Roystonia regia*) and the so-called sausage tree (*Kigelia africana*), as well as bamboo (*Bambusa vulgaris schr.*). The lignum vitae tree (*Guiacum officinale*) can also be found here. It is known locally as 'iron wood' because it is extremely hard and was therefore used in many of the sugar mills, the remains of which still dot the island.

EBENEZER METHODIST CHURCH

From the Recreation Ground walk down High Street, where busy vendors' stalls crowd the first stretch of pavements, or the parallel St Mary's Street, both of which lead to the quays. The latter would take you to **Ebenezer Methodist Church D**, constructed in 1839. Methodist teaching on the island was inspired by a prosperous plantation owner, Nathaniel Gilbert, who was a Speaker in the House of Assembly. Inspired by the preaching of John Wesley (1703–91) in England, he brought the message home to Antigua. The first chapel was built here in 1786, but so popular was Methodism that the congregation quickly outgrew the small building and a larger structure was needed. Unfortunately, the subsequent one was badly damaged in an earthquake in 1843 and again in 1974. On both occasions it was repaired, then in 1982 it was declared a historical landmark and work was carried out to strengthen the structure.

Historical though it may be, the exterior is not architecturally very interesting, and the building is usually only open when services are in progress (Sunday at 8.30am). It is sometimes used for other events and concerts, however, and if you pop in when one is

in full swing or being set up, you will find a pleasing, airy interior with a wide wooden gallery running around three sides.

NATIONAL MUSEUM

Down Long Street, past the Cathedral of St John the Divine, on the corner of Market Street stands the **Museum of Antigua and Barbuda** E (tel: 462 4930; www.antiguamuseums.net, Mon–Fri 8.30am–4.30pm, Sat 10am–2pm). The stone building, which was originally St John's Old Court House, was constructed in 1747 on the site of the first city market, and is the oldest building still in use in the city. It was designed by an English-born architect, Peter Harrison, and financed by a tax levied on local slave owners. The court of justice was held on the ground floor of the building and the upper floor was used as the Council and Assembly meeting room.

National Museum of Antigua and Barbuda

Established in 1985, the Historical and Archaeological Society of Antigua and Barbuda operate the museum. The fusty, old-fashioned layout tells the story of the island, from its geological birth to political independence in 1981.

There is a fine collection of Amerindian (mostly Arawak) artefacts, brought from various sites all over the island, and displays on sugar production – including a steam engine – and on the mid-19th century emancipation of slaves. Also on display is the cricket bat that belonged to Viv Richards; in 1986 he used the revered bat to score the fastest Test match century in history.

THE WATERFRONT

At the lower end of High Street is the former Bank of Antigua in two solid, pillared edifices on the left. On the right stands a

Cruise ship moored at Heritage Quay

small bronze statue of Vere C Bird, known as 'Papa Bird', the first prime minister and the most dominant figure in the island's political history (see page 18).

The compact waterfront is the main focal point of town, and approaching from this direction King's Casino (see page 92) will be your first introduction to **Heritage Quay F**.

Cruise ships crowds

With a steady increase in cruise ships calling at St John's, if possible, try to avoid the days they are in town. Not only are there crowds but the restaurants and shops often hike their prices when the passengers overwhelm the town.

The casino opened in 1988 and was built to cater to the needs of passengers from the cruise ships that call at the modern, 900ft (274-metre) dock that was constructed in St John's Harbour in 1988. Heritage Quay (see page 93), the adjoining duty-free shopping complex, grew up around the same time. When ships are in port, there is sometimes live steel band music playing here.

Next door to the dock, encompassing a whole block between St Mary's and Redcliffe streets, is the purpose-built, ochre-coloured **Vendors' Mall** (see page 93). Before the modern mall was built in 2001, stallholders occupied little wooden shacks that blocked access to nearby streets. Some of the lively hustle and bustle of a West Indian market has been retained in this more organised setting.

The waterfront boardwalk leads into the beautifully restored **Redcliffe Quay G** (see page 93), on Redcliffe Street. This is one of the oldest parts of St John's and in 1991 was awarded a prestigious preservation award, recognising it as an outstanding example of the rehabilitation of authentic West Indian Georgian architecture. This used to be at the very heart of the flourishing coffee, rum, sugar and slave trade between Europe,

Fort James

Africa and the island. It's an attractive development, with the well-restored, 17th- and 18th-century dockside warehouses converted into shops, restaurants and cafés, enhanced by vivid climbing plants and shady palm trees, and it has the atmosphere of a small island village.

South of the quay is a third dock, the Nevis Street Pier, which has increased the port's capacity for even more cruise ships to berth here.

From Redcliffe Street, turn right to find the **Heritage Market**  (see page 95), at the south end of Market Street. This vibrant vegetable and fruit market used to be held in the street, but is now housed in a high-ceilinged, purpose-built structure. Next door, in a smaller but otherwise identical building, is the Craft Market, selling locally made souvenirs such as banana leaf hats, rag dolls, carvings and beads. Right outside Heritage Market is a huge, audacious statue in honour of Vere C Bird, painted in colours that are vivid even for this tropical town.

THE NORTH COAST

Apart from the fort and two superb beaches, this coast does not have a great deal in the way of attractions, but there are some interesting corners and byways. For nature lovers the off-shore islands provide an engaging excursion, usually

visited by boat or catamaran trips that pick up visitors from St John's or from hotels all over the island.

FORT JAMES

North of St John's the road curves round towards **Fort Bay** and follows the sweep of a pleasant white sand strip, which has escaped the cruise ship invasions. It is very popular with local families at weekends and on public holidays, as it is the closest good beach to town. There are lots of refreshment, barbecue and souvenir stalls, in season, and loud music at weekends. In the early morning it is peaceful, with only locals standing chatting in the clear water.

From the beach, paths have been laid out among the trees leading to the remains of **Fort James** ❷ (always open). On a site originally called St John's Point, the fort was built, along with Fort Barrington (see page 68), to protect the entrance to the harbour from enemy ships and pirate incursions. The foundations were laid in the 1670s, a few years after the French had sacked St John's, but the walls did not go up until early in the 18th century.

◉ MORAVIAN MEMORIAL

At the end of High Street, in front of the casino, is the Westerby Memorial Fountain. It commemorates George Wall Westerby, Bishop of Moravia, who died in 1888 after 'labouring faithfully in the West Indies for nearly 50 years', as the inscription reads.

The Moravian sect began in Bohemia in the 15th century, resurfaced in Moravia in the 18th century, then spread to the Americas, reaching Antigua in 1765. The mission was to take the gospel to all oppressed people and provide both primary and secondary education for slaves. There are 11 Moravian churches on Antigua, all well attended by the devout islanders.

When it was completed it had 17 cannons, which were increased to 36 during the American War of Independence (1775–83) at the time that Britain got very edgy about the islands. The fort never engaged in battle but it must have been a successful deterrent.

The site is sadly neglected but 10 of the huge cannon remain, as do some of the original walls. Apart from the magnificent view, it is the size and the site itself that are the most impressive, and the battery of great guns facing out to sea.

RUNAWAY AND DICKENSON BAYS

Some of the **Runaway Bay** ❸ beach was eroded by Hurricane Luís in 1995, but it is still a very lovely bay with sun loungers and umbrellas to rent and a beach bar. The beach and sea views attract a sizeable number of visitors, particularly when the cruise

The Blue Waters Resort wedding gazebo

ships are in. Just inland, **McKinnon's Salt Pond** parallels the road and the beach and is a good place for birdwatching – sandpipers, terns, pelicans, herons and West Indian whistling ducks can all be seen here.

> ## Masons' stone
>
> A plaque on the wall of Fort James states that the first stone was laid by William Isaac Matthew, the Provincial Grand Master of the Three Lodges of the Free and Accepted Masons of Antigua.

The coast road to Dickenson Bay takes you via Corbison Point, which divides the two bays. Set high on a neat green bluff is a conical stone structure that at first sight could be a renovated sugar mill, but is in fact the remains of an 18th-century British fort. Fragments of Amerindian pottery have been found on this site, but no traces of any early civilisation are visible.

Running between Corbison Point and Weatherills Point, the mile-long sweep of **Dickenson Bay ❹** beach is almost unbelievably white, its waters stunningly turquoise-blue. Windsurfers and water-skiers love it, but there is also a protected swimming area so that they don't encroach on those who prefer to laze or swim. This is one of the most heavily populated tourist areas on the island, so it can get busy at the height of the season. The two main hotel-resorts here are the couples-only **Sandals Grande Resort** and the family-friendly **Halcyon Cove Resort** (see page 136). A short distance north of here is the **Blue Waters Resort** (see page 135), at Soldier Point; it is well known as a venue for weddings – the latticed wedding gazebo can be seen on the clifftop.

AROUND JABBAWOCK BEACH

Further around the coast is Beggars Point and **Jabbawock Beach ❺**. It is a totally natural spot that is popular with locals

Jabbawock Beach

and for windsurfing and kitesurfing. From both the point and the beach you can see **Prickly Pear Island** offshore, a five-minute boat ride that's extremely popular for daytrips.

Between Jabbawock Beach and **Camp Blizzard** stands the campus of the **American University of Antigua** (AUA), the most modern campus in the Caribbean. AUA provides a comprehensive modern learning facility for students aspiring to be doctors in the US and Canada; and all just footsteps from the beach!

Just south of here is the Antigua and Barbuda Defence Force's Camp Blizzard, housed in what was the US Naval Base. The US leased the land from 1941 until the early 1990s when they handed it back to the Antiguan Government. On the right of the gated entrance to the military camp there is an unpaved road that leads to **The Pottery** (Dutchman's Bay; tel: 562 1264; www.sarahfullerpottery.com; Mon–Fri 9am–3pm). Sarah Fuller makes and sells individually designed pottery using local clay and Caribbean

blue glazes. The terracotta clay is dug in the central plains of the island, air-dried and stored until it is needed. Many of the designs reflect the island's colourful history and indigenous features – sugar mills, pineapples and exotic blooms.

JUMBY BAY ISLAND

Along the airport skirting road, with Winthorpes Bay to the left, is the Jumby Bay ferry dock, which is the only access to the luxurious Jumby Bay Resort (see page 136). The island is in fact only 1 mile (2km) end to end and with less than a 4-mile (6km) circumference.

Jumby Bay is home to one of the greatest natural wonders on Antigua, the hawksbill turtle. Among the most endangered species of sea turtles, the Atlantic hawksbill (*Eretmochelys imbricata*) has always been prized for its beautiful shell and the jewellery that is produced from it. In 1987 the **Jumby Bay Hawksbill Turtle Project** ➏ (www.jbhp.org) was instigated, as people became aware of the valuable nesting ground here. This project is funded by the Jumby Bay Island Company and by private donations, along with assistance from the Odum's School of Ecology at the University of Georgia, which organises and co-ordinates the project.

According to the Wider Caribbean Sea Turtle Recovery Team and Conservation Network (WIDECAST), this nesting site is one of the most important

Failed plan

Rats have always been a problem on Antigua. Centuries ago, plantation owners introduced the mongoose to kill off rats that were attacking the sugar cane. Unfortunately, the plan didn't work and the island now has a surplus of mongoose too. The long, low creatures are often seen scuttling across the roads.

and best-studied rookeries of hawksbill turtles in the entire Caribbean region.

The team seeks to increase public awareness of sea turtles regionally and internationally through school visits and educational turtle watches for both residents and tourists. Young guests at Jumby Bay Resort can experience a turtle nesting at Pasture Bay and release hatchlings into the sea. Supervised turtle watching trips are available to all visitors between June and November by contacting the Environmental Awareness Group (tel: 462 6236; www.eagantigua.org). This is one of several eco projects undertaken by the EAG across Antigua and Barbuda.

FITCHES CREEK

South of the airport, **Fitches Creek** is an affluent neighbourhood on Fitches Creek Bay. Spreading out from the traditional village street are roads dotted with smart villas, their gardens overflowing with flowering trees and palms. **St George's Church** is located in a splendid setting overlooking Fitches Creek Bay. An Anglican church built in 1687 and remodelled some 50 years later, it was badly damaged by Hurricane Luís in 1995 but now restored. Dawn's Nursery, which has been operating since 1987, is down a left turn past the

Stained glass in Parham's St Peter's Church

Kitesurfer in action

church. Hibiscus, bougainvillaea, orchids and a wide selection of colourful tropical plants are on sale here, including indigenous species such as calabash, the silk cotton tree and passion fruit. Just north of the church, local artist **Gilly Gobinet's gallery** (www.gillygobinet.com; Nov–June Mon–Fri 9am–1pm) is located in her charming, secluded seafront property. Her original paintings, both figurative and abstract, are showcased in beautiful surroundings with stunning views over the water. She has a studio on the premises where you can see her at work and perhaps enjoy a drink in the courtyard.

PARHAM

Southeast towards Parham, the mill towers of Parham Hill Estate (a private estate not open to visitors) can be seen on the right, as can the tall, graceful royal palms surrounding the house. Royal palms were once associated with all the colonial

Great Houses on the Caribbean islands, usually lining the driveways. Parham Hill is one of Antigua's finest remaining examples. Built in 1689 for the wealthy Tudway family (who at one time also owned Guiana Island), it stayed in the family until the late 19th century. The house has been lovingly restored and repaired after damage by several hurricanes.

The colonial village of Parham features one prominent building, the Anglican **St Peter's Church** ❼, which was the first building in the village to be lit by electricity, in 1920. The present church is the third to be built on this site; the first, constructed in 1711, was a wooden structure that was burned to the ground, leaving only a walled graveyard in the open countryside. Interesting gravestones from some of the old island families remain in the overgrown churchyard. The

The North Sound waters are a snorkelling paradise

second church, built in 1754, was dismantled to make way for the present one, built in 1840.

This light, airy building is octagonal in shape and features a beautiful, ribbed, ship's keel ceiling and some of the original stucco work. It is one of the finest examples of Georgian colonial architecture in the Caribbean. The roof was damaged during Hurricane Hugo in 1989 and underwent major repairs in time for the 150th anniversary of its dedication, on 29 June 1990.

There are some pretty wooden houses and refreshment stalls in the village of Parham, but there is not much more. It was the first British settlement on the island and the home of one of the early British governors. Because of this, some people claim that it was the original capital, but this is not the case. Parham's sheltered port, the first on the island, flourished with the sugar trade, but today it only offers anchorage for a few pleasure yachts and a small fleet of fishing boats.

CRABS PENINSULA AND OFFSHORE ISLANDS

A little further on around the coast from Parham, the low, flat stretch of **Crabs Peninsula** comes to an abrupt end at the Antigua Defence Force military installation. Located on Crabs Peninsula is the government-owned Water Desalination Plant, built in 1987. Although most visitors will not get too excited about this, it is worth remembering that on an island that suffers from severe water shortages, it is desalination plants that enable hotels to provide warm showers and flushing toilets.

From the east of Crabs Peninsula, it is easy to see the islands that lie in North Sound. The largest is Guiana Island, separated from the mainland by The Narrows, a strip of water about 400ft (120 metres) across. They are all uninhabited and can be reached by boat. Small private charters can be arranged but most people see them from boat or catamaran

Deer legacy

Fallow deer were introduced to Guiana Island by the Codringtons in the 1730s to provide meat for their plantation workers. Their likeness can be found on the Antiguan coat of arms.

trips around Antigua's coast (see page 122).

The North Sound islands offer a rare opportunity to appreciate the glories of nature, both above and beneath the water. As you glide along in a boat you can look down and see small stingrays below. Some of the endangered species found in these islands include the West Indian whistling duck (*Dendrocygna arborea*), the tropical mocking bird (*Mimus gilvus*), the Antiguan ground lizard (*Ameiva griswoldi*) the red-billed tropicbird (*Phaethon aetherus*) and the hawksbill turtle (*Eretmochelys imbricate*).

Guiana Island ⑧ is believed to have been first occupied as early as 2,000 BC by Amerindians, but it was named after the English settlers who came here from Guiana (now Surinam) when it was occupied by the Dutch after the Treaty of Breda in 1667 and they were forced to leave. Sugar cane, cotton and staple provisions were grown by the English settlers in the early years, and the island was later taken over by Charles Tudway of Parham Hill. In 1812, it passed into the hands of Sir William Codrington, a member of one of Antigua's oldest landowning families, and it remained in the family until 1929.

Under the later ownership of Guiana Island Farms, a Welsh couple, Taffy and Bonnie Bufton, were brought to Antigua to manage the land, on which the main crop was cotton. When this was deemed unprofitable, the island was allowed to revert to nature and the Buftons remained as caretakers, looking after a herd of merino sheep, whistling ducks (now an endangered species on Antigua) and a herd of fallow deer.

There were at least 100 deer in the herd, some so tame they would eat from the Buftons' hands. Despite this, plans for a hotel development were proposed and the Buftons forced to leave. Mr Bufton died soon afterwards, but his wife moved into accommodation provided by the government.

Sadly, many of the deer disappeared. Occasionally fresh deer tracks indicate that some are still living there, but no one knows how many. The hotel development never took place and Guiana was left to go wild. The newly elected Antiguan government, however, signed an agreement in June 2014, just days after coming to power, with Chinese investors to build a major new development on the island and neighbouring Crump Island. Although ground has been broken, there is still strong opposition against the development, which if completed

Hell's Gate Island's spectacular coral archway

could comprise a golf resort, several five-star hotels, residential units, a casino and a marina, all enhanced by the island's beautiful beaches.

Great Bird Island ❾ lies to the north and is the next largest and the most popular for local people and visitors on day trips. There are two beautiful white beaches, on opposite sides of the island, and patches of coral reef surrounding it that make it a snorkelling paradise.

Great Bird is home to the red-billed tropicbirds, which nest on the cliffs on the eastern side of the island between December and June and are seen taking advantage of the wind currents as they fly in search of fish. They are easily identified by their flowing tail streamers, which are about half the length of the adult's body. Sometimes, however, their tail

⊙ ANTIGUAN RACER

Great Bird Island hosts what is believed to be the world's rarest snake. The Antiguan racer (*Alsophis antiguae*) is harmless and is being conserved by the Antiguan Racer Conservation Project (www.antiguanracer.org), whose mission is to conserve threatened coastal and marine species as well as this critically endangered reptile. When the project began in 1995, only 50 snakes were found but by 2014 their numbers swelled to around 1,000, so efforts are paying off. A major factor was removing rats from the island. The grey-blue females are slightly larger than the silvery-tan males, reaching just over 3ft (1 metre). Primarily feeding on lizards, the snakes are active in the early morning and late afternoon and often keep out of sight during the heat of the day. Those working on the project have now introduced the racer to several other local uninhabited islands.

The twin windmills at Betty's Hope

feathers are plucked off by aggressive frigate birds, which you will also see overhead.

Tiny **Hell's Gate Island** is especially interesting as it boasts a spectacular 20ft (6-metre) coral archway, formed by erosion. Just under the arch is a small pool with a sandy beach forming a natural swimming pool – you can swim here if the sea isn't too rough. It is said the island gained its name because the waters are only a few feet deep on one side of the arch, but plunge to great depths on the other side – almost down to hell. A number of rare birds nest on this island, including the brown noddy tern (*Anous stolidus*) and Zenaida doves (*Zenaida aurita*).

Despite its name, **Rabbit Island** is known not for its rabbits, but for a large resident population of nesting brown pelicans (*Pelecanus occidentalis*) living on the western side. There probably isn't a bird that gives more pleasure to the observer than the pelican as it glides soundlessly down to catch a fish.

Recognition

Betty's Hope was recognised by Unesco and awarded a grant in 1994. It received the 1996 Ecotourism Award for preserving the island's cultural, agricultural and industrial heritage.

From a protective distance on a boat off Rabbit Island, the pelicans can be seen tending their nests, feeding their young and pecking at neighbours. Pelicans nest in colonies and the nest space is determined by the distance that the bird can stretch towards it neighbour. Two to four eggs are laid at a time and both parents share the task of sitting on them until they hatch.

EAST OF THE ISLAND

The east of Antigua is the least developed part of the island. Most of the coastline lies along the rough exposed Atlantic with breezes blowing in directly from Africa. There are few hotels but numerous beautiful beaches, uninhabited islands, a coastline fringed by mangroves and one of Antigua's most interesting historical sites.

BETTY'S HOPE

A few miles inland, the village of **Pares** ❿ is a good place to start exploring the east side of the island. Along the roadside here you may see sweetcorn being roasted over a coal fire at open-air stalls. This Antiguan speciality has a crunchy, nutty texture and is well worth sampling whilst here.

Just east of Pares village, a marked dirt road leads to **Betty's Hope** ⓫ (tel: 462 1469; Mon and Wed–Sat 10am–4pm, opening times are somewhat erratic). This was Antigua's pioneer sugar plantation; established in the 1650s by Governor Christopher Keynall. It was one of the most prosperous plantations and

flourished (thanks to slave labour), for over 250 years. The estate was taken over by the Codrington family, who already had other plantations on Barbados. Christopher Codrington was Governor General of the Leeward Islands from 1700 to 1704, and the family owned nine other plantations in Antigua during the 18th century.

With the decline of the sugar trade the estate was allowed to fall into complete disrepair and many of the stones in the Great House were removed for use in local buildings. However, in 1990, the value of this site was realised, and a conservation project was initiated.

Part of the former estate has been allocated as a heritage site, and a museum and visitor centre occupy the former cotton house storeroom. One unique feature of Betty's Hope is that it had twin windmills, one of which has been successfully

Stingray City teems with marine life

restored, complete with sails, using some machinery and arte-facts gathered from other ruined mills on the island. On special occasions it can be seen in operation but even when not working it is still an impressive sight.

Perhaps more impressive – certainly more moving – is the brief, illustrated history of slavery described in the museum. This is one of the best places in Antigua to gain an insight into the sugar industry that made the island landowners so wealthy, and the slave trade that made it possible.

THE EAST COAST

North of Betty's Hope, on one of the east coast's many ragged peninsulas, **Seatons** ⑫ is a pretty village that straggles downhill towards the sea. It used to be a much bigger place but in the 1950s, after a severe hurricane, many villagers moved to Glanvilles (a short distance east along the main road) and founded a new village. Seatons used to live by fishing, but many of the fishermen now work in the tourist industry.

A scenic five-minute speedboat ride from Seatons will whisk you off to **Stingray City** (tel: 562 7297; www.stingraycityantigua. com), a shallow stingray pool with a white-sand bottom surrounded by beautiful coral reef where visitors can swim with native stingrays, spiny lobsters and other marine life.

The second attraction in Seatons is the half-day ocean-kayak trip run by **Paddles** (tel: 463 1944; www.antiguapaddles.com). This is a well-run, husband and wife operation that takes small groups of visitors on a motor boat from Mercers Creek to the near offshore islands within the North Sound Marine Park. There they propel their kayaks between the tiny islands, stopping every so often for an informative talk on the ecology of the mangrove vegetation that surrounds them. This is the habitat of shy turtles, stingray, starfish, parrot fish and a host of tropical birds. When

Devil's Bridge

thoroughly exhausted, the party gets back on the launch and are taken to Great Bird Island for a short hike to the top, then they are kitted out with snorkels for a spot of exploration around the coral reef or a swim off the tiny beach. After that, it's back to base for their famous nutmeg rum punch and banana bread on the patio.

DEVIL'S BRIDGE

About 3 miles/5km east from the Seatons at Indian Creek you will discover **Devil's Bridge** 13, a remote, wild site at the end of a narrow promontory. The area is known as Indian Town Point, although no archaeological remains have ever been found here that showed evidence of Indian settlement.

The 'bridge' is a remarkable example of wind and salt-water erosion, which has formed a natural arch, approximately 30ft (10 metres) long by 7ft (2 metres) high, carved in the lime-stone rocks by the waves rolling in from Africa, some 3,000

The royal poinciana tree blooms in June and July

miles (5,000km) away. There is a blowhole that produces an impressive spout of sea water, rather like that of a whale. The waters surrounding it are always rough, pounding against the coast, and the rougher they are, the more impressive the spout. Do not be tempted to get too close to the ocean or try to walk across the arch as it can be very dangerous, depending on the tide.

Some say Devil's Bridge gained its name because desperate enslaved Africans from nearby estates would commit suicide by throwing themselves from it into the sea, so local people would say, 'the devil have to be there'. Legend has it that if you throw two eggs into the water to boil, the devil would keep one and return the other.

ST PHILIPS

Back inland, just before the dirt road to Betty's Hope, a road takes you south through **St Philips** ⑭. There isn't much to the village, but **St Philip's Church** is worth a stop. The first parish church was established here in 1690 and then rebuilt in 1830. Hurricane Luís took the roof off this one in 1995, but it has been replaced with green roofing. Judging by its smart new red roof, the house next door most probably suffered a similar fate.

The church is a pleasing, stone-built structure, with tall windows allowing lots of light inside, usually only open for

services on Sunday, but the churchyard is a peaceful spot, and the view over Willoughby Bay is not only beautiful, but atmospheric. Even on a calm day it is easy to imagine hurricane force winds whipping across the water, threatening the exposed buildings on the clifftop.

Just past the church, by a small pond in a field on the right, is more evidence of the dangerous power of Hurricane Luís, and the regenerative powers of nature. The 100ft (30-metre) Hurricane Tree refused to give up when it was felled by the winds in 1995. Sprouting fresh green shoots, it still grows in this horizontal position.

The ruins of Montpelier Sugar Factory, reputed to have been one of the finest in the Caribbean in the 1890s, lies on the outskirts of the village, although there is not much to be seen from the road.

There are breathtaking views of Willoughby Bay from the coast road heading east. A narrow viewing point has been created on the

⊙ POINCIANA

Usually known as 'flamboyant' or 'flame trees', Poinciana are an unforgettable sight often seen along the roadside in full bloom in June and July, covered with dazzling bright red flowers. The tree, a native of Madagascar, is umbrella shaped and offers generous shade. Well adapted to drought, it blooms profusely then loses its leaves during the dry season, appearing almost dead, but as soon as the rains come new growth begins. The seed pods are long (up to 2ft/50cm) and when dry make a distinctive rattle. They are popular as percussion instruments, locally called shack shacks (rattlers). You will see varnished versions of them for sale in souvenir shops throughout the island.

Half Moon Beach

roadside to allow for photo opportunities and to encourage drivers to keep their eyes on the road ahead and avoid a less attractive fate.

Just over 2 miles (3km) northeast of St Philip's is the lively, well-cared-for village of Freetown. As its name suggests, this was one of the first free villages established on the island after emancipation in 1834 (Freemans and Liberta are two of the others).

HALF MOON BAY

Just south of Freetown you will find one of the most beautiful beaches on the island – although there are many other contenders for the title. The crescent-shaped light pink and white sands of **Half Moon Beach** ⑮ rank among the top beaches in the world. At one end there are rolling waves, wonderful for surfing and windsurfing, at the other a coral reef shelters a calm bay, perfect for swimming and sunbathing. The hotel on the south side of the bay, which closed down after Hurricane Luís hit in 1995, is being transformed into a luxury resort and is due to open in 2021. On the path down to the sand you'll find Beach Bum bar (see page 110), serving simple Caribbean food.

For the fit and adventurous, there's a walk starting just beyond the hotel that will take you along the beach and over the sharp-edged cliffs to Soldier Point where there is a natural coral bridge poised high above the crashing waves. The scenery

is spectacular, and you are unlikely to meet another soul along the way. Further north towards Nonsuch Bay, just off the coast is the deserted **Green Island** ⑯, which offers white sand beaches waiting to be discovered. It is an ideal spot for snorkelling and a common stop for sea charters and excursions, which can spoil the tranquillity when several arrive at the same time.

ENGLISH HARBOUR AREA

Largely dominated by the old naval dockyard, which was so important in carving out the maritime history of Antigua, this far south peninsula commands the most historical interest. Ruined fortifications occupy a commanding position on high ground from which there are spectacular views over

Horseshoe-shaped Falmouth Harbour

the coastline and English Harbour. Today, the area boasts a leading marina where luxury crafts ply the waters around Falmouth Harbour and many world-class yacht races are held. Here also is one of Antigua's most glorious beaches, laid out before a lush backdrop of steep hills and forest.

FALMOUTH

Built around a lovely natural harbour, the township of **Falmouth** ⓱ was the first English settlement on the island, but the town is small and unprepossessing today. Horseshoe-shaped **Falmouth Harbour** has a beautiful hillside backdrop. The marina was built to cater for luxury mega-yachts and there are several docks where craft are moored, spread out across this lovely stretch of water. A walk along the jetty is a draw for anyone interested in sailing

The brick pillars are the only remains of the old Boat and Sail Loft at Nelson's Dockyard

or those wishing to spot a gin palace; the marina also hosts the Antigua Sailing Week.

Perched high on Monk's Hill, watching over Falmouth Harbour, are the remains of **Great George Fort**. The site was chosen in the 1680s as the perfect location to guard Falmouth from the French, who had recently attacked St Kitts. The work was completed around 1705, but the fort

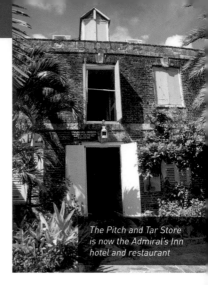

The Pitch and Tar Store is now the Admiral's Inn hotel and restaurant

was never engaged in battle. Like many of the historic sites in Antigua, this one is in need of care and conservation.

A diversion west from here to **Rendezvous Beach** ⑱ is well worth the effort. As you drop down to the palm-fringed turquoise waters you will soon realise why this is considered to be one of the most magnificent beaches on the island. A four-wheel drive vehicle is a great way to arrive at this beach, alternatively on horseback from the nearby **Spring Hill Riding School** (see page 88). Since 2014, the bay has been under development and in the near future you may well have to share this once isolated beach with a residential community and boutique hotel.

English Harbour lies further south of Falmouth where you will find Antigua Yacht Club and several bars and restaurants. A narrow road continues to **Pigeon Point**, with pristine sands and breathtaking views of Falmouth Harbour. For fine dining on the beach, French-owned Catherine's (see page 110) is a must.

Dockyard Museum

NELSON'S DOCKYARD NATIONAL PARK

English Harbour, Antigua's graceful and evocative historic district, is focused on the 15 sq miles (38 sq km) of Nelson's Dockyard National Park, a Unesco World Heritage Site. Almost all the park's other sites of interest overlook the harbour and incorporate Clarence House and Shirley Heights.

Nelson's Dockyard ⑲ (tel: 481 5021; www.nationalpark santigua.com; daily 8am–6pm; entrance fee includes Shirley Heights and Dow's Hill Interpretation Centre) is the only operational Georgian naval facility in the world, and has been preserved and beautifully restored as a National Park in 1985. You enter through a covered market area where souvenirs and crafts are on sale and you can buy freshly squeezed fruit juice.

The dockyard dates from 1743, although most of the preserved buildings were constructed towards the end of the 18th century. Its purpose was as a careening station, where British

ships were scraped, repaired, and restocked with water and supplies. The harbour on which it sits was originally chosen as a hurricane haven in the 1670s for the ships that protected the West Indian colonies from enemy attack.

Horatio Nelson (neither Lord nor Admiral at the time) was in command here from 1784 to 1787. Nelson's brief was to enforce the Navigation Acts, which prohibited direct trade between the newly independent states of America and the British colonies. He took his task so seriously that he managed to alienate everyone concerned, and his stay in mosquito-ridden English Harbour – 'this infernal spot', he once called it – was not a happy one.

By the late 19th century, steam power had taken over from sail, and the facility gradually became irrelevant, finally closing in 1889. Renovation work began in the 1950s, and the dockyard reopened in 1961. It is once again a working harbour, and one of Antigua's biggest tourist attractions.

The first building you come to used to be the Pitch and Tar Store, and is now a hotel and restaurant, **Admiral's Inn** (see

☉ TREES IN THE DOCKYARD

Nelson's Dockyard is well planted with flowering trees and bushes, among them the lignum vitae, known as iron wood because the timber is so hard. It used to be widely used for boat building, and in the construction of sugar mills. The coconut tree (*Cocos nucifera*), which has the largest seed in the world, is also identified. Next to the Admiral's House is a tree believed to be more than 200 years old. The sandbox tree was so called because its dried pods were filled with sand and kept on the officers' desks, where they used it in place of blotting paper to dry wet ink on documents.

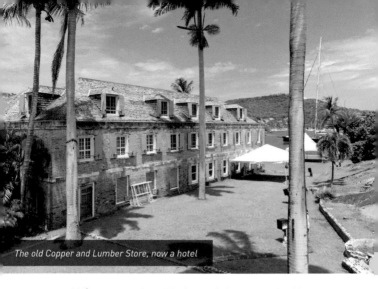
The old Copper and Lumber Store, now a hotel

page 111), very popular with the yachting fraternity. Next you come to a rectangle of huge brick pillars; they once formed the lower floor of the Boat and Sail Loft.

As you continue along the main path you will pass a number of buildings (most have helpful information boards outside) before reaching the **Admiral's House**, which is now the interesting **Dockyard Museum** (daily 9am–5pm), with a figurehead of Nelson over the door; a gift shop, library and research centre are also housed here. Although the house was built for the commanding officer (in 1855, long after Nelson's time), no admiral ever spent a night here. The Admiral's Kitchen, set back from the museum, is now the Dockyard Bakery, where freshly baked pastries can be purchased.

The original **Copper and Lumber Store**, close by, has also become an attractive hotel and restaurant (see pages 110 and 138) and the pub next door is also a good place to eat.

Many buildings now have commercial functions: Dockyard Divers (www.dockyard-divers.com) operates from the Old Guard House; some unique shops and galleries occupy other historic buildings, and here too is a beauty salon. A path behind the Copper and Lumber Store leads around the dinghy dock to **Fort Berkeley**, on the headland. Only ruins remain, but they are atmospheric, and well worth visiting. The guard house has been restored and the original powder magazine, which had the capacity to store 300 barrels of gunpowder, can be seen. From the fort, which was the first defensive point built to guard English Harbour, and named after Admiral James Berkeley, First Lord of the Admiralty, you get a good sense of what the whole complex was about.

Across the mouth of Galleon Bay, now a haven for some splendid yachts, a chain used to be stretched to prevent small enemy boats entering the harbour. It was joined to Fort Charlotte on the far side, but the latter, destroyed by an earthquake in 1843, is now only identifiable as a pile of rubble.

If you are feeling really fit and energetic you could continue up the track (turn off just before Fort Berkeley) to the sparse ruins of Keane's one-gun battery and the remains of Fort Cuyler, which looks south towards the French island of Guadeloupe. When it was built in 1798 by

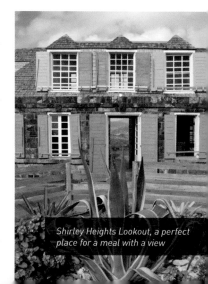

Shirley Heights Lookout, a perfect place for a meal with a view

Pillars of Hercules

At the foot of the hill on which the Shirley Heights Lookout stands is a striking sandstone formation known as the Pillars of Hercules. The rocks are a challenge to get to by land – there is a strenuous walk from Fort Charlotte at Galleon Beach but you need to keep an eye on the tide – so the best way to see them is from the water.

General Cuyler there were four 32lb (14.5kg) guns, and when one was fired in 1799 the platform sank seven inches (18cm). There are spectacular views from here, and the fort clearly demonstrates the strategic importance of this piece of land.

From Nelson's Dockyard a narrow road winds uphill to **Clarence House** (not open to the public). Built for Prince William, Duke of Clarence (1765–1837), it has a superb situation overlooking the harbour. Formerly the residence of the governor-general of Antigua, it fell into disrepair but has been saved by a restoration project. The late Princess Margaret and the Earl of Snowdon spent their honeymoon here in 1960, and Prince William, Duke of Cambridge, stayed here when he served as a midshipman.

Past Clarence House a track to the left leads to **Dow's Hill Interpretation Centre ⑳** (daily 9am–5pm but can change seasonally; included in the National Park entrance fee), built with the aid of a grant from the Canadian Government. There is a café and gift shop at the centre and a 15-minute multimedia presentation, which illustrates Antigua's history with illuminated tableaux and television screens.

The great thing about the Interpretation Centre is its situation. It stands among the ruins of the house built in the 18th century for General Alexander Dow, which was destroyed by the 1843 earthquake. From the belvedere the

view over the dockyard, English Harbour and idyllic Galleon Beach is quite spectacular.

SHIRLEY HEIGHTS

From the Interpretation Centre the road winds uphill along The Ridge to **Shirley Heights** ㉑. A left fork takes you to the **Blockhouse**, on top of Cape Shirley, Antigua's most southerly point. From here you look down on the palatial house and grounds owned by musician Eric Clapton, and on **Indian Creek**. In the distance, Mamora Bay and the immense sweep of Willoughby Bay can also be seen from here.

Back on the main track, the first structure you reach is the well-preserved ruin of the **Officers' Quarters**, on the right. Opposite them is the military cemetery, where the many victims of yellow fever were buried. A few gravestones and memorials still stand on the blustery clifftop.

The road now comes to an enforced halt at **Fort Shirley**, named after General Sir Thomas Shirley, governor of the Leeward Islands from 1781–91. One of the ordnance buildings has become **Shirley Heights Lookout**, a deservedly popular bar and restaurant, famous for its Sunday barbecue, steel bands and reggae (see page 89).

Snowy egret

There is an outdoor seating area at the back, from where the panoramic views are superlative.

BETHESDA TO POTWORKS DAM

The road that runs east from Falmouth Harbour offers a rewarding detour down to **Mamora Bay**, which marks a southern peninsula with the Caribbean Sea on one side and the Atlantic Ocean on the other; on the edge of which perches the exclusive **St James's Club Resort** (see page 139). From Mamora Bay, the road meanders along the coast with yet more wonderful views over Willoughby Bay and then turns slightly inland to Christian Hill and **Bethesda ㉒**. The biblical-sounding village got its name from one of the first schoolrooms opened in the Caribbean for the education of slaves, in May 1813; the name means 'hallowed'.

The beautiful beach at Hawksbill Resort

Today, Bethesda is more often visited for the nearby Donkey Sanctuary (www.antiguaanimals.com/donkey; Mon–Sat 10am–4pm, free but donations appreciated). Located on an unmade road (less than a mile down on the left), the sanctuary offers a permanent home for

> ### Birdwatching at Potworks Dam
>
> Among the birds seen at Potworks Dam are the osprey (*Pandion haliaetus*), the snowy egret (*Egretta thula*) and the West Indian whistling duck (*Dendrocygna arborea*).

neglected donkeys. Run by the Antigua and Barbuda Humane Society, it currently shelters more than 150 donkeys and is a very popular attraction for children. Informative and passionate staff will introduce you to the friendly animals and kids are invited to groom them. The Humane Society also offers an 'Adopt a Donkey' programme, which provides visitors with a photo of their donkey and an official adoption certificate.

On the northern outskirts of the village is the **Bethesda Tamarind tree**. It is easy to spot as it is the largest tree beside the road (on the left on a slight curve) and painted white around the base. The tree has a symbolic meaning for Antiguans.

In 1951 a number of workers on the sugar estates went on strike over rates of pay. Union leaders insisted that no work would be done until the matter was resolved, even though the employer stated that he would starve the strikers into submission. The workers and their families suffered enormous hardships and were reduced to living off what natural resources they could harvest from land and sea, but in the end they won the dispute, despite military intervention and imprisonment for some of their leaders. In January 1952 the sugar workers were awarded a 25 percent wage increase and went back to work. The tamarind tree at Bethesda was the site of one of the meetings

Fort Barrington

between the two sides as they attempted to thrash out their differences, and has become a symbol of the workers' struggle.

Further north the road leads around the eastern side of **Potworks Dam** ㉓. Potworks Dam is named after an 18th-century pottery owned, like so much else on the island, by the Codrington family. It was officially opened in May 1970, after the need for it had been recognised for some time.

During several periods of severe drought, Potworks has been a life-saver in the past but as limited rainfall increases Potworks Dam has been known to run dry. Shortage of water is a problem on Antigua, one which means that much agricultural land is not being fully utilised and the island cannot be self-sufficient in terms of fresh produce, some of which has to be imported from neighbouring islands. The area attracts a wonderful variety of birdlife and is of great interest to bird-watchers, especially around the western edge.

WEST OF THE ISLAND

The west is the most lush and loveliest part of the island, and the area with the most elevated ground. Its highest point is Mount Obama, formerly known as Boggy Peak, and renamed in 2009 in honour of the US President. It is also the most developed part of the island, with the most resort hotels, renowned for their stunning beaches.

WEST OF ST JOHN'S

A short distance outside St John's, sitting on a piece of land jutting out into the Caribbean Sea, **Five Islands Village** ㉔ is named after five tiny, rocky islands at the other side of the eponymous harbour. This is a large and lively village with plenty of small shops and bar shacks and neatly dressed children on their way to and from school. There was apparently no settlement here at all at the time of emancipation (1834), but by 1842 a village had grown up around a **Moravian church**.

Beyond Five Islands Village the road to Galley Bay is very rough and in wet weather it is often impassable by car. The road winds uphill to a turning area that provides a panoramic view from Deep Bay to St John's Harbour, and as far as Dickenson Bay (see page 37) in the distance. You may also spot the wreck of the Andes, a cargo ship that sank in 1905, lying in only 20ft (6 metres) of water in Deep Bay. Because it is so

Sir George's Old Battery

For those seeking a challenging hike, the ruins of Sir George's Old Battery are on Fullerton Point to the south, but they are not easy to reach. The battery is prominently shown on maps of Antigua, but little remains. The location is impressive, though.

Kayaks for rent on Jolly Harbour beach

shallow, the wreck makes an excellent snorkelling site. The **Galley Bay Resort** (see page 140) is an enchanting hideaway, which occupies 40 acres (16 hectares) of tropical gardens, with a lagoon and bird sanctuary, and a secluded palm-fringed beach.

South of here stands the **Hawksbill Resort** (see page 140). It is a serene, attractive place, with villas and apartments set out in luxuriant grounds. There's a small pool and several pretty beaches (one clothes optional), with sea kayaks lying invitingly on the white sands. From the beaches you can see, approximately half a mile (1km) offshore, the **Hawksbill Rock** from which the complex took its name. The large rock does look very much indeed like the head of a hawksbill sea turtle.

FORT BARRINGTON

Back up the coast is the Grand Royal Antiguan Resort (being refurbished under new ownership after years of standing empty), marking the edge of lovely **Deep Bay**. Standing on a promontory on the far side of Deep Bay, in an area called Goats' Hill, are the ruins of **Fort Barrington** ㉕. You can walk along the beach at Deep Bay to get to Goat Hill and then it is a steep but short scramble up the footpath to the circular remains on the top of the little hill. The first fort was built here in the 1650s

to guard St John's Harbour. Fort James, begun a couple of decades later, stood guard on the other side. The ruins are redolent of the island's maritime history, and the views from this lonely spot are spectacular, especially at sunset.

AROUND GREEN CASTLE HILL

Inland, about 4 miles (6.5km) south of St John's, is the 565ft (172 metre) **Green Castle Hill** ㉖. This grassy hill is the remnant of an isolated volcano. There are large rocks and boulders, so-called megaliths, scattered around the southwestern summit of the hill, which some like to associate with ancient pagan rites, although there is no evidence to back this up. There is also a large stone plaque at one end of the summit, commemorating Lord Baldwin, Governor of the Leeward Islands from 1947–49, whose ashes are buried beneath it. The climb to the top of Green Castle Hill starts from Emanuel village and takes about 45 minutes, but it is not particularly steep or difficult and the views from the top make it well worth the effort.

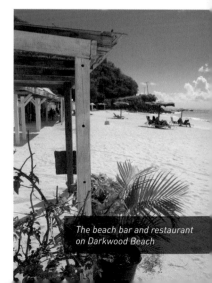

The beach bar and restaurant on Darkwood Beach

On the west side of Green Castle Hill, back on the main road from St John's, at the village of **Ebenezer** the 87ft (26 metre) broadcasting and telecommunications

antenna installation can be seen on the top of Mount Obama. The next village is **Jennings**, which began as a small estate owned, in 1749, by Samuel Jennings. Later in the 18th century the acquisitive Codrington family bought the land, but by the time of emancipation in 1834 it had changed owners again. The Moravian church then established a school here and the village of Jennings sprang up around it.

One of the greatest pleasures of visiting these villages, and many others around the island, is the opportunity to witness how the ordinary people of Antigua actually live. Strung out along the road are brightly painted wooden houses, known as chattel houses, a term left over from the days of slavery. In season they are smothered with bougainvillaea, hibiscus and other bright blossoms, while banana palms offer shade outside. Sometimes you have to look closely to distinguish between a house, a shop and a bar.

THE JOLLY DEVELOPMENTS

Just outside Jennings at the westernmost point of Antigua, is **Pearns Point**, now the site of what is considered one of the top real estate developments in the world. It comprises of a low-density, environmentally sensitive construction with seven spectacular beaches.

Further south the landscape opens up and, after there has been some rain, becomes pleasantly verdant. A series of conical, wooded hills and, beyond, some lofty palm trees, announce that you are approaching the coast. The road here passes the Christian Valley Agricultural Station, home to Antigua's collection of mature fruit trees, on the left and the tiny Caribbean Lighthouse Radio Station on the right, before **Bolans** village and the large **Jolly Beach Resort** (see page 140) and **Jolly Harbour** complexes.

The two Jollies initially share a driveway but straight ahead is Jolly Beach, a resort hotel spread along an idyllic beach on Lignum Vitae Bay (named after the hardwood tree) and to the right is Jolly Harbour. The latter has a sheltered harbour, a smart marina, commercial centre with shops, banks and restaurants, and a large Epicurean supermarket, plus an 18-hole golf course and other activities. By the beach is the popular Castaways restaurant, all set among the villas and apartments that are available for sale and rent.

A short distance south is the picturesque, red-roofed **Our Lady of the Valley** church, which stands opposite a mangrove pond. Here the antics of pelicans, egrets and noisy, long-legged avocets, locally known as darling birds, can provide entertainment from the road, or more comfortably from

Turner's Beach enjoys a beautiful setting near Johnson's Point

Cades Bay Pineapple Station

Valley Church Beach. The beach lies beyond the mangroves, separated by a neatly tended expanse of grass. The only drawback of this idyllic beach is that it can become overcrowded with cruise ship passengers at times.

On a bluff sit the pretty villas of **Cocobay Resort** (see page 139), followed by a succession of gorgeous white beaches. **Ffryes Bay** is very popular with locals and visitors alike. It offers plenty of parking and is an ideal spot for a picnic or barbecue.

DARKWOOD BEACH

The next beach round is **Darkwood Beach** ㉗, regarded by many as one of the best beaches on Antigua and the setting is beautiful. The only development in the immediate vicinity is a beach bar and restaurant, which has been here since 1975, making it the oldest beach bar on the island. It can get busy and many people choose to bring their own picnic. From Darkwood Beach, and several other spots along here, you can see the neighbouring volcanic island of Montserrat. The floating waterpark just offshore is a hit with kids.

Just south is **Turner's Beach**, It's lively here with seafood restaurants (lobster is a speciality) and local art for sale in a shop across the road. Turner's Beach Restaurant (see page 113), in a pink and green chattel house, is a busy spot during

the peak season. Try to avoid visiting on days when the cruise ships are in town as the serenity is spoilt.

Nearby other beach bars and restaurants include Jacqui O's Beach House (see page 112), one of the most popular beach restaurants in Antigua. The place is known for its friendly service, excellent lunches and dinners. OJ's beach Bar along the same road is also worth a stop (see page 113).

TOWARDS MOUNT OBAMA

Continuing along the coast, the little village of **Urlings** has a flourishing fishing community. Off **Cades Bay**, the longest reef on the island, Cades Reef, ensures calm waters for swimmers and is great for snorkelling. You will notice black pineapples, the national fruit of Antigua, for sale on stalls along the road. These

Old Road is, unsurprisingly, the oldest village on Antigua

fruit, which are unique to the island, are grown at nearby **Cades Bay Pineapple Station**. You can see the plantations from the road, and the interesting thing about these pineapples – apart from their colour and especially sweet taste – is that they grow at ground level, with the palm-like fronds sitting on the soil.

From Cades Bay, a road leads towards **Mount Obama** ㉘, the highest point of the island, at 1,319ft (402 metres), a part of the Shekerley Mountain range. It is now a national park and there are various jungle trails for hiking. Formerly known as Boggy Peak, it was renamed in honour of former US President Barrack Obama. The road up to the summit is only suitable for 4 x 4 vehicles and is not for the faint-hearted; it is very steep and not well maintained. It is possible to walk up and the views from outside the fenced area are pretty stunning.

On the far side of shallow Morris Bay, the exclusive **Curtain Bluff Resort** (see page 139) stands out. One of the most

◎ FIG TREE STUDIO ART GALLERY

Situated in the heart of the rainforest in the gardens of artist Sallie Harker, the Fig Tree Studio Art Gallery (tel: 460 1234; www.figtreestudioart.com, Nov–June Mon–Sat 9.30am–5.30pm) is a delightful gallery that showcases original artwork from all over Antigua and the wider Caribbean. You will find paintings evoking the wonderful light and colour of the region, featuring rainforest, seascapes, flora and fauna. There is also superb craftwork, created from the natural environment, using materials such as driftwood and seashells, and plant life picked from the rainforest. Also featured is pottery, hand-blown glass jewellery and a range of items made using materials washed up on the seashore.

Antigua's rainforest has plenty of trekking trails

expensive resorts on the island, it has an enviable position, as there are calm and peaceful waters on one side of the bluff, and good surfing waves on the other.

Old Road 29 is the oldest village on the island, and one of the liveliest. The original settlers of 1632 recognised the advantages of the deep-sheltered **Carlisle Bay** (now renowned for snorkelling), on which it sits, as it provided them with anchorage safe from storms and pirate attacks ('road' was a nautical term for anchorage). St Mary's church here is the oldest on the island.

The landscape along this stretch of coast has now become far more green and fertile, and the village is a mass of tumbling bougainvillaea, frangipani and poinsettias, as well as bananas and giant ferns. Keep your eyes open for a huge, hollow-trunked silk cotton (kapok) tree (*Ceiba pentandra*). You may also notice people selling huge conch shells on roadside stalls, along with black pineapples and tropical juice drinks.

Antigua Rainforest Zip Line Tours offers an array of hair-raising activities

FIG TREE DRIVE

The road then turns inland and winds through what is known as **Fig Tree Drive** ㉚. The first thing to remember is that there are no figs – it is an Antiguan word for bananas. And there are plenty of bananas along here, as well as mangos, guavas and soursops. Also, another large-scale producer of the indigenous black pineapples, **Claremont Farms** (www.claremontfarms.com), can be found here.

Simply driving along the road gives a taste of this magnificent area of the island, and the only part that is mountainous and covered in truly tropical vegetation. This is Antigua's rainforest region and as you drive through the lush landscape you see nature in its most natural form.

Just off Fig Tree Drive in **Wallings Forest** you will find an exciting activity, **Antigua Rainforest Zip Line Tours** ㉛ (tel: 562 6363; www.antiguarainforest.com, Tue–Sat 9am–2pm;

pre-booking required), which offer a range of tours involving zip line and rope challenges, aerial walkway bridges, tree houses, scary vertical descents and challenge courses. An exhilarating experience is the forest canopy; suitable for all adrenalin junkies starting as young as four years. Safety is of paramount concern, with helmets and harnesses imperative. There is also a gift shop and café-bar.

For those who prefer to keep their feet on the ground **Footsteps Rainforest Hiking Tours** (tel: 460 1234; www.hiking antigua.com) offer walks to Wallings dam and reservoir, and a climb up Signal Hill.

Back on Fig Tree Drive is little John Hughes village, and then the village of **Swetes**. The latter's chief claim to fame is as the birthplace of the former West Indies fast bowler, Curtley Ambrose. Off to the left, between the two villages, a path leads to Body Ponds, a series of dammed ponds where some peaceful walks can be enjoyed.

BARBUDA

A visit to Antigua would not be complete without a trip to its tiny sister island, Barbuda, which is about 62 sq miles (160 sq km) in area and lies some 30 miles (48km) northeast of Antigua. Devastated by Hurricane Irma in September 2017, this island, with its breathtaking coral-fringed, pinkish sands, crystal-clear water and charming leisurely pace of life, is working hard to rebuild and restore it to the beautiful paradise it was.

Irma decimated around 90 percent of the island's infrastructure with homes, schools, churches, medical facilities and boats destroyed. By early 2018 only about 360 people – the population is around 1,800 – had returned to the island and most

Rare birds

Only one chick per pair of frigate birds is hatched, and it remains in the nest for eight to 10 months, one of the longest dependency periods of any bird species. Because of this, they only breed every other year, which is most unusual in the bird world.

were living in make-shift tents or in rough accommodation still without power and running water. By the end of 2018 the first hotels and guesthouses were up and running and tours were departing regularly around the island. Getting there from Antigua is simple either by plane or ferry boat (see page 121).

CODRINGTON

A short taxi ride from the ferry dock brings you to the small town of **Codrington** ㉜ named after the original English land-holders and Barbuda's main settlement. Most of the island's population lived here before the 2017 hurricane hit and the settlement is gradually finding its feet again. From here there are organised boat trips to the Codrington Lagoon. You can also take other tours to fabulous beaches and fascinating caves. Cars and bikes are available for hire from Codrington if you prefer to go it alone.

FRIGATE BIRD SANCTUARY

Prior to hurricane Irma a huge colony of frigate birds (*Fregata magnificens*) could be found on the 12-mile (20km) long **Codrington Lagoon** west of the town, one of the largest in the world; the lagoon was declared a National Park in 2005. Here, on the eastern shore is the **Frigate Bird Sanctuary** ㉝, once home to more than 10,000 frigate birds, which travel between the Caribbean and the Galápagos Islands. The area was decimated

by the 2017 hurricane, destroying the mangrove swamp, home to the nesting birds but gradually the birds are returning to nest in large numbers once more. Some 170 different species of birds visit the lagoon, including ibis, herons and kingfishers.

On the sea-side of the lagoon, **Palm Beach** ③④ is a magnificent 12-mile (20km) sweep of sand, snowy white in places, pink in others. Heading north is 11-mile Beach and continuing north is the new Barbuda Belle luxury hotel (see page 141).

MARTELLO TOWER

About 3 miles (5km) south from Codrington, the 56ft (17-metre) **Martello Tower** ③⑤ is the most intact part of the ruins of the River Fort. It is a popular spot for weddings. Close to the tower is the River Wharf Landing, where passenger ferries to and

Martello Tower

from St John's, load and unload. To the west is Palmetto Point, a popular location for surfers, while heading east along the coast are the eco-friendly Barbuda Cottages (see page 141). Continuing east is pristine Princess Diana Beach and beyond Coco Point, the site of the luxury Coco Beach Lodge, which was virtually destroyed in the hurricane. The lease has been taken over by the Discovery Land Company who are rebuilding the Barbuda Ocean Club on the site.

SPANISH POINT

On the southeastern tip of the island lies **Spanish Point** ❸, where there is one of the most beautiful beaches imaginable – **White Bay Beach**. Just to the northeast of Spanish Point, shown on most maps as **The Castle**, the sparse ruins of what was a lookout tower, for defence against attacks by Carib Indians, remain. Its strategic position means that it offers a fabulous view.

⊘ ROYAL SEAL OF APPROVAL

On Barbuda you can follow in the footsteps of the late Princess Diana. Barbuda was a favourite sanctuary of the Princess and the young Princes William and Harry. During the 1990s, she would find solace in the beauty of the island while William and Harry played happily on the powdery soft sands. The young family stayed at the prestigious K-Club Resort, which is now sadly abandoned and in 2019 became the subject of a legal battle over the building of a huge new development. Admired by the locals, the stretch of beach beside the K-Club was renamed 'Princess Diana Beach' in her honour during a ceremony on 1 July 2011, the day she would have turned 50 years old.

Cooling off at Codrington pier

THE HIGHLANDS

On the east side of the island lies an area called the Highlands – although they are not particularly high. There is little development and the land is wilder. Here, the fallow deer that the Codringtons introduced roam freely, along with wild boar, red-footed tortoises and whistling ducks. There are several caves in the area; some are not accessible and some should not be explored alone, but it is easy to arrange for a guide.

HIGHLAND CAVES

Dark Cave 37 is in the middle of the Highlands about 4 miles (7km) east of Codrington, and just south of Darby's Sinkhole. The cave has a narrow entrance leading to a vast cavern containing pools of water and is a popular habitat for several species of bats.

Darby's Cave 38, a sinkhole not far from Rubbish Bay, is reached via a (driveable) dirt track from Codrington, then a

The north shores of Barbuda

40-minute trek with a guide. The sinkhole has vertical, cliff-like sides and is around 70ft (22 metres) deep and 300ft (92 metres) in diameter. It is surrounded by lush vegetation and a number of tall trees grow in the cave, with their tops at eye level. The path drops precipitously and sunlight filters through the trees and vegetation. There is an abundance of bird life in the dark interior, which resembles a tropical rainforest. A 30ft (9-metre) overhanging cliff has formed stalagmites of calcium carbonate.

Indian Cave 39, the most interesting prehistoric site on Barbuda, is located at Two Foot Bay on the northeast coast. From the main entrance there is a short, narrow passage and two small Amerindian petroglyphs (rock drawings) can be seen as the passage opens into another cave where daylight filters in. The Amerindian people used rock drawings to guard their caves and the people in them from evil spirits. These are the only ones known to exist in Antigua or Barbuda. For guides or tours see www.barbudaful.net.

HIGHLAND HOUSE

The highest point on this flat island, about 3 miles (5km) from Codrington, is just 120ft (37 metres). The ruins of **Highland House** (known locally as Willybob) can be found

here. The house was built at William Codrington's request in the 1720s, and the overgrown remains of the stables, a water cistern and part of an aqueduct are still visible. The most interesting thing about the place, however, is the view, which is quite spectacular.

Since Hurricane Irma, issues with the government of Antigua over land ownership in Barbuda have resulted in ongoing court cases, and until these are resolved the future for Barbuda, its tourism development and its people cannot be fully determined. Will Barbudans be able to develop their island in the way they wish and not be subject to mass tourism or outside interference? For further information on Barbuda and the latest developments email Claire Frank at barbudaful@gmail.com (www.barbudaful.net).

Sunset on the beach

Antigua hosts an annual Sailing Week

WHAT TO DO

Despite their physical dissimilarities, Antigua and Barbuda share a lively patois, a vibrant Carnival tradition, and long-established, animated music and sporting occasions. The advent of tourism has undoubtedly encouraged the latter, and boosted special events such as the annual Sailing Week. Cricket and sailing represent the mainstay of the sporting calendar, providing the perfect excuse to party throughout the year.

SPORT AND RECREATION

Recreation in Antigua and Barbuda generally takes place on or under the water and there is a plethora of reputable companies who organise trips and tours (see page 122). Cricket holds a very special place in all Antiguans' hearts, which is very evident across the island, but there are also many other sports and activities you can take part in if you prefer to remain on dry land.

WATER SPORTS

Beneath the surf, diving and snorkelling opportunities are spectacular. Fringing barrier reefs, caverns, walls and over 300 wrecks in Antiguan and Barbudan waters provide a wealth of adventure, matched by the abundant aquatic life. Nurse sharks, parrot fish, eels, stingrays and lobsters are common sights along Cades Reef, The Chimney or around wrecks such as the *Andes* and the *Jetias*.

Diving and snorkelling shops abound in every bay, many of which are based at hotels. At English Harbour, **Dockyard Divers** (tel: 729 3040; www.dockyard-divers.com) offer a wide range of options, from introduction to diving and one-day courses to a range of PADI courses. As well as courses for certified divers,

Both islands are snorkelling heaven

Indigo Divers (Jolly Harbour, tel: 562 3483; www.indigo-divers.com), welcome beginners, too.

Surfing and paddle boarding are highly popular in the frisky waters off the east coast and among the more sheltered bays of western waters.

Sailing is also very popular on Antigua and there are numerous organisations that arrange packages for those who want to join in the fun. At English Harbour, **Nicholson Yacht Charters** (tel: 460 1530; www.nicholsoncharters.com) and **Antigua Yacht Charters** (tel: 07879 815458; www.antiguayachtcharters.com) are both well-established reputable companies.

Most resort hotels have water sport facilities, including water-skiing, kayaking and sailing dinghies, and some will hire to the public; **Blue Waters** and **Jolly Beach resorts** (see page 140) offer day passes for use of their facilities.

Further out, chartered deep-sea fishing trips will land tuna, wahoo, kingfish and dorado. **Mystic Amara III** (tel: 464 7112) are a company based at Jolly Harbour and offer trips suitable for both beginners and experienced anglers.

CRICKET

Worshipped by hoards of adoring fans, the national sport is played informally all year round on both Antigua and Barbuda,

the official season running from January to July, when domestic leagues flourish, inter-island competitions are fought and the West Indies team hosts international rivals.

Since the demise of the Antigua Recreation Ground (see page 28) in St John's, Test matches are played at the **Sir Vivian Richards Stadium** (tel: 481 9200; for details of upcoming matches www.cricschedule.com/venue/antigua.php) in the North Sound area east of St John's – the venue of several matches during the Cricket World Cup in 2007.

OTHER ACTIVITIES

Antigua has two 18-hole golf courses, the **Cedar Valley Club** (tel: 462 0161; www.cvgolfantigua.com) just outside St John's and at **Jolly Harbour** (tel: 462 3035; www.jollyharbourantigua.com). Both are challenging courses with carts for hire and lessons available.

Hiking in Antigua can be extremely challenging with the heat and blazing sun to contend with. Remember to wear a hat, put on sun block and take plenty of water with you. You can enjoy the many hiking trails by yourself, or with organisations such as the

⊙ CRICKET MANIA

Cricket was introduced by the British in the early 19th century and remained an élite game for many years, but was taken up and perfected by sugar plantation workers. The Rising Sun Cricket Club in St John's was the first to be established for working-class people, in 1920. Living legend and 'Master Blaster', Sir Isaac Vivian Alexander Richards, is worshipped as the greatest local hero. He captained the West Indies XI during some of their finest years and scored the fastest Test century on his home ground against England in 1986.

Environmental Awareness Group (www.eagantigua.org) that organise regular hikes. **Footsteps Rainforest Hiking Tours** (tel: 460 1234; www.hikingantigua.com) take two-hour hiking tours through the valuable rainforest conservation area. Cycling around the islands can be very rewarding, albeit a bit bumpy.

Spring Hill Riding School, near Falmouth Harbour (tel: 773 3139; www.antiguaequestrian.com) is the Headquarters of the Antigua and Barbuda Horse Society. It offers lessons and horseback treks to Rendezvous Bay, where you can paddle in the sea with your horse.

Antigua is well served with spas and lifestyle related salons. Most beach resorts have their own first-class spas but there are also some good independent options such as **Akparo** (tel: 460 5705; www.akparo.com) at Nelson's Dockyard. In addition to traditional treatments like soothing mud wraps and deep-tissue massages, several spas offer ancient techniques such as reflexology and Reiki. Some specialise in Caribbean-inspired treatments using local ingredients including coffee, seasalt and calcium-rich seaweed. Lots of spas also come with excellent fitness facilities, and some even have dedicated instructors offering yoga and pilates classes.

Mountain-biking in Shirley Heights

ENTERTAINMENT

No trip to Antigua or Barbuda would be complete without experiencing calypso or soca at a party, the echo of a steel band or the Carnival. Antiguans love to party and music and festivals go hand in hand – weekly parties are advertised all over

Soca

Soca meaning 'soul of calypso' originated in Trinidad and Tobago. It is a fusion of East Indian and calypso music, created to appeal to the masses when calypso music was threatened by the more popular reggae music.

the island. Look out for flyers, newspaper, radio or television announcements promoting 'bashments' (dances) for dancehall, reggae or the ubiquitous retro nights at bars and clubs. *Merengue* and *bachata* batter the airwaves of several nightclubs and bars. Most hotels and beach clubs regularly hold ticketed beach parties, offering music, food and drink and late-night seaside revelry.

SPECIAL EVENTS

The **Shirley Heights Lookout** (tel: 728 0636) comes alive every Sunday when it is the site of one of the most lively events on the island, the Sun 'Jump Up'. A huge outdoor barbecue takes over from the restaurant's kitchen, and crowds of tourists and Antiguans throng up the hill to party and listen to steel bands (4–7pm) and reggae (7–10pm). The main event is a natural one – the sunset, an unforgettable sight.

Antigua Sailing Week attracts over 200 boats and 5,000 crew members from all corners of the globe. Centred on Falmouth, the week combines serious racing with outrageous parties; wet T-shirt contests, greasy poles and hedonism 'lively up' the waters

Carnival is the highlight of the Antiguan calendar

of the fifth largest sailing regatta in the world. In preparation during the week leading up to this extravaganza, drinks are chilled for the Antigua Classic Yacht Regatta. Historic yachts gather to race, while a heritage festival onshore keeps landlubbers amused.

Nothing matches **Carnival** in terms of charisma, entertainment and energy levels. At the end of July into August, music and festivities erupt over all St John's, with smaller-scale sprees scattered across the island to coincide with the festivities. Not to be outdone, calypso and soca have been fused from Trinidadian sounds, while reggae, dancehall and steel bands add to the musical ensemble, drumming up the crowds at Carnival City, better known as the Recreation Ground in St John's. Barbuda has always had its own Carnival (Caribana Festival) in June but this was cancelled in 2018 in respect of those who lost everything to hurricane Irma. Its future is uncertain due to funding. For more information on special events, see page 97.

NIGHTLIFE

Nightlife in Antigua can mean many things, from beach bars where you can have a drink and enjoy the tropical sunset, to romantic restaurants, glitzy casinos, nightclubs or sports bars. If you want local nightlife, you can just hang out in bars and listen to steel bands, reggae or US imports such as hip hop and R&B. If you're a Brit feeling homesick, there are English pubs with darts and pool tables. Many restaurants have lively bars, some with live music and there is regular live music in the resort hotels.

Dickenson Bay is the number one hotspot on the north coast. **Ana's on the Beach** (tel: 562 8562; www.anas.ag) is a chic restaurant and bar where you can dance on the sand. **BeachLimerz** (tel: 562 8574; www.beachlimerz.com) is a celebration of music and local cuisine just steps from the turquoise waters of Fort James Beach; reggae, calypso and jazz rhythms combine with the cocktails to stir your soul.

If you're feeling mellow make for St John's and the quaint **C&C Wine House** (tel: 460 7025; www.ccwinehouse.com) at Redcliffe Quay, where Cutie and Claudine will welcome you with a glass of South African wine.

Jolly Harbour is where it's all happening on the west coast of Antigua. **The Sugar Club** (tel: 484 3702; www.sugarridgean-tigua.com), at the Sugar Ridge Hotel, is a great place for live entertainment, or enjoy a rum cocktail overlooking the marina at the **Crow's Nest** (tel: 562 2637). Apart from serving authentic Caribbean food and great cocktails, **Castaways Beach Bar** (tel: 562 4446; www.castawaysbeachclub.com), nestled on the white sands of Jolly Beach, always has various live music playing and is good for fun party nights and special events.

The bars of English Harbour are always overflowing with sailors. In Falmouth the **Skullduggery Café** (tel: 463 0625; www.skullduggerycafe.com) is much loved for its espresso

martinis. At Life on the Corner on Dockyard Drive (tel: 722 0020) you can enjoy a drink on the terrace or kick back on the sofas with friends for a cocktail. The music volume increases around 10pm with every genre of music to dance to or just chill out. Part of the Antigua Yacht Club Marina complex, **Cloggy's** (tel: 460 6910) is popular for its food by day but as the evening wears on it becomes a lively late-night drinking hole that draws a yachting crowd.

Don't miss **Abracadabra** (tel: 460 2701; www.abracadabra-antigua.com), just outside Nelson's Dockyard, an elegant Italian restaurant early in the evening that transforms into a pulsating outdoor nightclub later.

Gambling compulsions can be appeased at Antigua's flashy **King's Casino** (tel: 462 1727; www.kingscasino.com, Mon–Sat 10am–2am, Sun 6pm–2am), which is always pulsating with locals and tourists. Located at Heritage Quay in St John's, the casino offers an array of gambling choices, including roulette, Caribbean stud poker, blackjack and state-of-the-art video-poker as well as a wide selection of slot machines.

Jewellery for sale

If you fancy an evening at the flicks, the **Caribbean Cinemas** megaplex (tel: 562 4000; www.caribbeancinemas.com) on Friars Hill Road, just

five minutes from St John's, boasts eight screens showing the latest films and food and drink options.

SHOPPING

WHERE TO SHOP

The first place to head when it comes to shopping in St John's are the dockside duty-free shopping complexes. At **Heritage Quay** and **Redcliffe Quay** (www.historicredcliffequay.com; Mon–Sat 9am–6pm, and Sun when cruise ships are in dock) you can buy leather bags at **Vera Pelle**, arts and crafts at **Zemi**, hand-made jewellery from **Goldsmitty**, clothing from independent boutiques such as **Shylo**, **Zeitgeist** and **Noreen Phillips Couturiere**, as well as locally made ceramics, cool linen clothes and beads and bags. Note: you may be asked for your passport and proof of return date if purchasing duty-free goods.

Retaining the lively hustle and bustle of a West Indian market, **Vendors' Mall** has been purpose-built for the job. On the ground floor, open to the street, are stalls run by local vendors, selling craftwork, colourful sarongs, beads, bracelets, and T-shirts.

On the outskirts of St John's, along Friars Hill Road, several mini-malls have sprung up, including the **Woods Mall**, which offers a large variety of retail therapy. The island's largest supermarket, **Epicurean**, is set back off Friars Hill Road; modelled on a US-style supermarket, it has everything one could wish for, as well as a full drug pharmacy.

Warri

Restricted largely to resident specialists, the game of warri has clear links with almost identical board games in West Africa. It is played in bars, on verandas or on street corners, using a wooden board as the base on which players aim to capture their opponent's counters.

WHAT TO BUY

Shopping in St John's

Shopping in Antigua can be divided into two distinct categories. One comprises the duty-free goods that can be bought at Heritage Quay in St John's. The other category includes more specifically Antiguan goods that make attractive gifts or souvenirs, such as batik, pottery and paintings by local artists and wood carvings. All these goods can be found in Redcliffe Quay and in shops at the large resort hotels.

Individually designed pottery, which often captures vivid sea blues and original patterns and glazing styles, is available to buy at various outlets. **Sarah Fuller** (see page 38) works out of her Coolidge Studio using local clay and Caribbean-inspired designs. On the main road in English Harbour, the **Rhythm of Blue Gallery** (tel: 562 2230; www. rhythmofblue.com) is the showroom for Antiguan born Nancy Nicholson, who digs the clay for her distinctive one-of-a-kind pottery here on the island.

Antigua has an active artist community, and the work of leading local artists' is displayed and sold in shops and galleries right across the island. Intuitive or landscape scenes style the bulk of the painters' output. **Gilly Gobinet's** colourful Caribbean subjects in watercolour and acrylic fill her studio at Fitches Creek, while the **Fig Tree Studio Art Gallery** (see

page 74) showcases and sells lots of regional art. See www.antiguanartists.com for a list of Antiguan artists.

Other souvenirs worth bringing home include herb-scented soaps, Carib coffee, fiery pepper sauce, guava jam, bottles of sea moss and, of course, the local speciality, Antigua rum.

MARKETS

St John's **Heritage Market** (Mon–Sat until 6pm), at the south end of Market Street, is a vibrant vegetable and fruit market housed in a high-ceilinged, purpose-built structure. It is best visited early on Friday or Saturday morning when it is at its loudest and busiest.

Colourful, fragrant tropical fruits and vegetables are in abundance here; look out for juicy mangoes, papaya, pineapples, star fruit, custard apples, sweet little bananas (locally called figs) and guava. You may also see the root vegetable dasheen, breadfruit and plantain filling the wooden stalls. Often the market stocks a mixture of locally grown food and produce imported from nearby Dominica and other islands where tropical fruit is more easily grown because of the higher rainfall. There are also several stalls selling bright tropical flowers – ginger lilies and antirrhinums, again imported from Dominica.

Next door, in a smaller but otherwise identical building, is the Craft Market, selling locally-made souvenirs, such as banana leaf hats, rag dolls, beads and carvings.

ACTIVITIES FOR CHILDREN

Antigua is a wonderful place for children. Aside from the natural attractions and organised entertainment, children are very popular with the locals, who are particularly kind to them.

Cricket on the beach

The amazing number of outstanding safe beaches Antigua and Barbuda have to offer has to be one of the greatest draws for those arriving with children. With this comes the opportunity to take part in numerous water sports – everything from kayaking and sailing to water-skiing and snorkelling are on hand. There are many boat excursions that will appeal to children, whether onboard a catamaran or island hopping with a chance to see some of the islands' amazing sea creatures.

Accessible from Seatons, **Stingray City** (see page 50) is an amazing experience – not just for children – and kids will delight in being able to pet the friendly donkeys at the **Donkey Sanctuary** (see page 65), near Bethesda. In the hills of the rainforest off Fig Tree Drive, the **Rainforest Zip Line** (see page 76) offers something a bit more exhilarating for slightly older children.

Neither of these two islands has much in the way of museums to drag kids around, but **Nelson's Dockyard** will entertain them with its sea-battle connections that will excite the imagination.

Additionally, the great benefit of staying at an all-inclusive resort is the number of organised children's activities available as part of the package.

CALENDAR OF EVENTS

January Minival: New Year's Day parade through the streets of St John's.

February Jolly Harbour Valentine's Regatta: five days over the Valentine's weekend; sailing, entertainment and partying.

March Wadadli Sound Festival: showcases the island's sound-system culture. Top DJs spin their decks for a large young crowd at Fort James.

April Antigua Sailing Week: world-renowned sailing regatta over five days, commencing at the end of April; welcomes participants from all corners of the globe, www.sailingweek.com.

A&B International Kite Festival: a popular family event held annually around Easter; colourful creations take to the sky off the north coast.

Antigua Classic Yacht Regatta: seven days of racing mid-April with spectacular vessels on show; hosted by Antigua Yacht Club at Falmouth Harbour, www.antiguaclassics.com.

May Run in Paradise: a half marathon held at the end of May attracts runners from around the world, www.runinparadise.com.

July A&B Mango Festival: unique annual festival celebrating the mango fruit, culminating in the Mango Pineapple Culinary Competition showcasing the islands most talented chefs; held at the Christian Valley Agricultural Station near Jennings.

July/August Antigua Carnival: one huge two-week party in the streets of St John's; at the opening parade people dance behind steel and brass bands dressed in colourful costumes; events culminate in a massive street party called J'ouvert on the first Monday in August, www.antiguacarnival.com.

August Seafood Festival: entertaining tradition held at Urlings Wharf, Carlisle Bay; competitions, boat rides, live music performances, local crafts, not to mention everyone's seafood favourites.

November A&B Independence Festival: celebrating Antigua's independence on 1 November 1981; a week of competitions, parades, expos and food fairs.

Gemonites Mood of Pan Festival: annual two-day festival showcasing the steel pan; takes place at the Dean William Lake Cultural Centre north of St John's; an opportunity for the young to showcase their talent.

December Nelson's Dockyard Old Year's Night Party.

EATING OUT

Antigua offers a wide variety of culinary options, from authentic Caribbean and specifically Antiguan dishes, to those with strong European influences. Although many visitors will dine in their all-inclusive resorts where they are likely to find international food served with distinct Caribbean differences, trying local food is an enjoyable part of any holiday, and Antigua has a lot of specialities not to be missed. Discover tempting street food, rustic rum shops, seaside eateries and village restaurants. The food is not excessively spicy, although hot pepper sauce can be found on many restaurant tables.

Take your pick of restaurants and cafés on Antigua, there are literally hundreds catering for both tourists and the local trade: there's everything from upmarket dining rooms to laid-back beach bars where you can enjoy a casual lunch or drink. Don't expect a quick turnaround, it's all about going with the leisurely flow here and remember that a 10 percent service charge is usually added to the bill. Meanwhile, Barbuda restaurants are very limited and, unlike its cosmopolitan neighbour, may have to be booked in advance. Restaurants are often closed out of the tourist season, so call to see if they are open before you go.

WHAT TO EAT

Culinary influences

The earliest settlers to the islands survived on a limited number of indigenous foods including sweet potatoes, black pineapples, plantains, maize, bananas, coconuts and beans. The surrounding ocean yielded a plentiful supply of fish and a myriad of seafood. There were few land animals so meat

was not a major part of the local diet.

The Arawak people were the first to introduce organised farming, cultivating the staples that are still so important today, namely maize and sweet potatoes. They also began to trade with neighbouring islands. Finally defeated by the Caribs in the 12th century, there was a gradual introduction of European influences, first with the early Spanish settlers and

Coconut Grove restaurant, Dickenson Bay

then with the coming of the British in the mid-17th century, who were responsible for bringing African slaves to their sugar plantations. From Europe the introduction of animals saw the diet supplemented with beef, milk and cheese. The African influence was less influential as the slaves lived mainly on a diet of rice but this would prove to be a substantial part of the menu in the following centuries, right up to the present day.

The 20th and 21st centuries have brought with them an influx of international ethnic foods, and 'foreign' Chinese, French, American and Italian restaurants have been springing up across Antigua for years.

Fish and meat

Fish and shellfish are abundant in Antigua, although lobster is usually expensive. There are however, plenty of fresh ones on the menu in Barbuda as they are native to Codrington Lagoon

and are an island delicacy. Conch (pronounced konk) is served in salads or as fritters – great, either way. Red snapper, king fish, grouper, swordfish and mahi mahi (dorado), and wahoo, which has a tuna-like taste and texture, are all good. Lobster is usually barbecued and served Creole-style with rice and spices.

Chicken and spare ribs are the most commonly eaten meats and both may be served with a spicy Creole sauce. You can find excellent barbequed chicken on the streets around St. John's and English Harbour. Jerk meat dishes, originating from Jamaica, are now also popular in Antigua. Meats on the restaurant menu include beef, pork, baked chicken, stewed lamb and goat. Beef and lamb are often imported from the US or Argentina, but goat, pork and chicken are produced locally.

Fruit and vegetables

Antigua is one of the driest of the Caribbean islands, which means that some fruit and vegetables have to be imported from Dominica and other islands. But a number of exotic varieties are grown here. Breadfruit, dark green on the outside

⊘ FARMING

Although tropical fruit is grown on the island, there is no major crop to replace the sugar monoculture. Sweetcorn, tomatoes, and root vegetables such as sweet potatoes, dasheen and eddo are the main vegetable crops. There is some cattle farming, but herds of sheep and goats are more commonly seen throughout the island, often wandering across the road, and devouring everything they can find. Goat is a staple food for the islanders, but given their numbers, it is surprising that it does not appear on restaurant menus more frequently.

with yellowish flesh, is full of vitamins, and mainly used as a vegetable – dull when boiled, good when baked or fried. Several varieties of fresh chilli are found in the markets and some are very fiery. The edible roots dasheen and eddo are used like potatoes; while callaloo, a leafy spinach-like vegetable, can be a side dish or made into soup. Pumpkin and okra are widely used, as is sweetcorn, and tomatoes, all of which burst with flavour.

Red snapper often pops up on the menu

A wonderful selection of fruit is available in season (May–October): mango, watermelon, guava, papaya (paw paw), passion fruit and, of course, bananas and plantains. The latter look like large bananas but have to be cooked – fried, boiled or ground into a flour – and are served as a main course side dish. And don't forget coconuts, which grow on the tall palms. On the beach, vendors will split and sell them to you with a straw so that you can drink the milk inside. Many of these fruits are also crushed into juice or used to make ice cream, jams and jellies. The indigenous black pineapple – which is not actually black but dark green on the outside when at its most delicious – grows in the southwest of Antigua, and is unique to the island. This small pineapple weighing about 1.2lb (1kg) is extra sweet and it's a delicacy that should be tried if you see it on a restaurant menu or on sale in a local market. It

Soursop

Soursop is a large green fruit with a prickly skin. They can be as much as 8 inches (20cm) long and weigh up to 6lbs (nearly 3kg). Although the fruit may be eaten raw, it is more often made into soft drinks, mousse and ice cream. The drinks tend to be over-sweetened, but the mousse and ice cream are delicious.

takes pride of place as the national fruit and sits proudly on the top of the country's coat of arms.

Specialities

Here are some local dishes that regularly pop up on menus and are well worth trying:

Antiguan butter bread – a soft buttery loaf of bread often served with cheese for breakfast.

Bull-foot soup – also known as cow-heel soup, made with the lower extremities of the cow and vegetables. It is really the gelatinous tissue between and around the joints of the feet of the animal.

Coconut soup – worth sampling for the novelty.

Ducana – The huge leaves of the coccoloba tree are used to wrap a mixture of spiced and grated sweet potatoes, coconut and flour; when cooked, the leaf is discarded.

Fungee (also spelled foongee and fungi) – a mixture of corn-meal and okra, similar to Italian polenta, and usually eaten with fish or meat.

Goat water – an unappetizing name belies a hearty stew full of flavour from goat seasoned with hot peppers, cloves and cinnamon.

Johnny cakes – a kind of doughnut, usually served at breakfast with salt fish.

Pepperpot stew – a tasty mixture of beef or pork with okra and pumpkin and sometimes dumplings.

Rice and beans speaks for itself and can be very good.

Roti – patties filled with curried potatoes, chicken or beef.

Salt fish – often served with fungee or in a tomato and onion sauce – a favourite for breakfast.

Sous – pork cooked with lime, onions, peppers and spices.

Desserts

If you can bear to drag yourself away from the amazing array of fresh fruits on offer there are other desserts and pastries that may tempt you. Conventional ice cream and locally-made American-style ice cream are readily available but there is also a small band of devotees creating traditionally made ice cream featuring a range of unusual flavours. Using fruits only when in season, the flavours include soursop, golden apple, coconut and even sweet potato. Drop into Fred's Belgian Waffles and Ice Cream in Redcliffe Quay in St John's and you will see ice cream and sorbets made on site in a multitude of luscious flavours. Other popular desserts include apple pie, plus pineapple and mango pie in season, and jelly – known here as jello.

Fungee and pepperpot stew are local specialities

Neighbourhood bakeries make a range of pastries at reasonable prices, featuring cookies, muffins, cakes and tarts. Local confectionery includes peanut brittle; tambran

Johnny cakes are a popular choice for breakfast

(tamarind) balls (the original sweet and sour); sugar cake coconut squares; and home-made fudge.

WHAT TO DRINK

Alcoholic drinks

Think Caribbean, think rum, and Antigua and Barbuda are no exception. The best local option is English Harbour Premium Rum, aged in oak casks for a minimum of five years, making it a great drink and a perfect gift to bring home. The local Cavalier rum is a light golden colour and usually forms the base for numerous mixed drinks. Nutmeg is used a lot, and is good grated onto rum-based drinks. One of the highlights of any trip to the islands is the ubiquitous rum punch made up of lime juice, syrup, rum, water, fruit juices or ginger ale, or as they say in the Caribbean 'one of sour, two of sweet, three of strong and four of weak'.

Sensational cocktails come in a myriad of flavours. Many of the resort hotels have their own signature cocktails, mixed by slick-handed bartenders. Popular rum-based cocktails include the Mojito, where your rum is blended with mint, lime juice and soda water; the Cuba Libre, a marriage of rum and cola; the strawberry Daiquiri, combining sugar, lime juice, white rum, fresh strawberries, a few drops of strawberry liqueur and lots of ice; and of course, not forgetting the ever-popular Pina Colada, with its rum, pineapple juice and coconut cream.

Beer is widely consumed on the island. The most common brands are the local Wadadli, from the original Arawak name for Antigua, Jamaican Red Stripe, Carib from Trinidad and some American and European brands. Wine is not so readily consumed by the locals, but imported wine is available in all resort hotels and most restaurants. Spirits, aside from rum, are not so popular with locals, but are easily obtainable.

Soft drinks

For quenching your thirst in the heat of the day nothing is more refreshing than the local freshly-squeezed fruit juices. Choose from mango, passion fruit, guava, tamarind, pineapple, coconut, banana, lemongrass and more. Non-alcoholic cocktails are just as inventive as their stronger counterparts and are a highlight of any day. Other popular local drinks on the islands are ginger beer, coconut milk and lemonade.

Local specialities include:

Mauby – based on tree bark and sugar, plus spices and often aniseed.

Peanut Punch – a shake made with peanuts or peanut butter, milk and sugar.

Seamoss – a type of seaweed, which is dried, then boiled and blended with milk, ice, and sweeteners such as cinnamon, sugar, vanilla, and/or nutmeg.

Sorrel – made with the bright red flowers of the

Celebration

Ponche Kuba Cream Liqueur, a thick creamy tan-coloured drink of lightly spiced rum-based cream, is a popular Christmas tipple in Antigua and Barbuda. Served chilled, neat or over ice, it is very sweet and smooth and often strengthened with the addition of brandy or more rum.

Cheers on the beach

hibiscus plant, which are boiled and then strained, cooled, and sweetened.

Soursop Juice – drink made from this local fruit.

Ting – a home-grown, sparkling grapefruit drink.

Tea, although available, is not overly popular. Coffee is the hot drink of choice. En route to Falmouth, a right turn down an unpaved track leads to the Carib Coffee Bean Company, which has been operating here since 1997. Estate-grown Arabica coffee beans are imported from the Caribbean Basin and parts of Latin and Central America and freshly roasted daily. This is the only such operation on the island and the aroma from the roasting beans lets you know that you are buying the freshest coffee available. Choose from their wide selection of coffee blends including the imaginatively named Hurricane Brew, Dark and Stormy, One Luv, Caribbean Dream and Tropical Morning Blend. Experience the process on their Open Roast Days (Nov–Apr Wed; www.caribbeancoffeeroasters.com).

PLACES TO EAT

We have used the following symbols to give an idea of the price for a three-course meal per person without drinks.

$$$ over US$55
$$ US$25–55
$ below US$25

ST JOHN'S

Alligators Bar & Restaurant $$ *Lower High Street, tel: 562 6289*. Concealed in a beautiful courtyard garden, the local chef at Alligators delivers simple food with a Caribbean flair, all freshly made and cooked to perfection. The curried goat is popular. Daily 8am–11pm.

Captain's Table $$ *Harmonites Steel Pan Yard, Point Fishery Wharf, tel: 562 3474*. The seafood here never disappoints; from the grill try locally caught mahi mahi, swordfish or wahoo or from the kettles, conch soup and clam chowder. Daily specials will excite your taste buds. Mon–Sat lunch only.

C&C Wine House $$ *Redcliffe Quay, tel: 460 7025*; www.ccwinehouse. com. Hidden away in a romantic courtyard, this delightful restaurant pairs excellent wines with tasty coconut shrimp, pastas, burgers, paninis and daily specials, all prepared fresh to order. Mon–Sat 11am–11pm.

Harbour View $ *Redcliffe Quay, tel: 562 8381*. Enjoy a cappuccino, glass of rum, panini, salad or opt for a full meal at this delightful café that is ideal for watching the action from an elevated vantage point looking out over the harbour. Daily 9am–5pm.

Hemingway's $$ *St Mary's Street, tel: 462 2763;* www.hemingwayantigua. com. Tuck into Creole cuisine and fresh seafood dishes while people watching from the wrap around veranda of this fabulous green and white wooden building. Daily 8.30am–11pm.

Lion Pavilion $$ *Colesome Farmers Market, Jonas Road tel: 728 3328.* This brightly painted family-run eatery serves modern and creative vegan dishes using organic produce grown on the family farm. Dishes are cooked in jabba clay pots and the menu changes daily. Mon–Sat 9am–7pm.

Roti King $ *St Mary's Street and Corn Alley, tel: 462 2328.* This cracking little shack is the best place for roti (a flour pancake or wrap filled with curried meat or seafood). Take a seat in the simple café and wash the food down with a glass of ginger beer (with a splash of rum). Mon–Sat 5–10.30pm and sometimes during the day.

Stella Ristorante $$ *Sunset Lane, tel: 789 7725.* Tree-house style restaurant set on the hillside with beautiful sea views over Runaway Bay. The Italian chef creates tasty cuisine ranging from pizza cooked in the wood-burning oven, to specials such as octopus carpaccio and lobster thermidor. Mon–Sat 6–10pm.

Touloulou Bar & Restaurant $$ *Marble Hill Road, McKinnon's, tel: 562 8778;* www.touloulo[urestaurant.com. Dedicated to Asian fusion cuisine, fabulous dishes journey from South East Asia to Thailand, Indonesia and the Philippines. Coupled with a lovely setting and attentive staff, this is an experience you'll want to repeat. Mon–Fri 11.30am–10.30pm, Sat 6–10.30pm.

THE NORTH COAST

Ana's on the Beach $$ *Dickenson Bay, tel: 562 8562;* www.anas.ag. Come through the pink doors for a Mediterranean-inspired menu. A typical meal could be Venetian seafood soup followed by red snapper infused in rosemary and garlic, rounded off with Caprese cake (chocolate almond). Daily 11am–10pm.

Bay House Restaurant $$ *Trade Winds Hotel, Dickenson Bay, tel: 462 1223;* www.twhantigua.com. With stunning views over the bay, the Bay House serves innovative cuisine such as blackened mahi mahi with crab sauce and parsley crushed potatoes and lobster in season. Daily breakfast, lunch and dinner.

Le Bistro $$$ *Hodges Bay, tel: 462 3881*; www.antigualebistro.com. This is probably the most elegant independent restaurant on the island, whose French menu includes the likes of fresh snapper fillet braised in ginger wine sauce laced with leeks or rack of lamb in mustard crust. Tue–Sun 6.30–10.30pm.

La Bussola, $$ *Rush Night Club Road, Runaway Bay, tel: 562 1546*; www.labussolarestaurant.net. Dine on a shady terrace listening to the lapping waves in this family-owned Italian restaurant. Seafood Italian style includes shrimp risotto and fishermen's spaghetti, plus delicious thin-crust pizzas. Interesting Italian wine selection. Mon–Sun 6.30–11.30pm.

Cecilia's High Point Café $$ *Dutchman's Bay, tel: 562 7070*; www.highpointantigua.com. This is a pretty wooden restaurant right on the waterfront. With Cecilia's Swedish influence, the menu has some interesting innovations. There is also an excellent wine list. Just five minutes' drive from the airport. Food served Fri & Mon noon–9pm, Sat & Sun noon–4pm.

Coconut Grove $$ *Dickenson Bay, tel: 462 1538*; www.coconutgroveantigua.com. On the beach next to Siboney Beach Club, this open-air restaurant specialises in seafood with a European flair. Try deep-fried shrimps with coconut flakes or jerk pork with tamarind sauce. Lovely for candle-lit dinners or laid-back lunches. Daily 7am–11pm.

The Cove $$$ *Blue Waters Resort, Soldier's Bay, tel: 462 0290;* www.bluewaters.net. This special occasion venue is dramatically set on a cliff and offers a tantalising menu of Caribbean and French dishes cooked with flair. Flaming torches lead onto the candlelit dining room with terrace from where there are mesmerising views. Dinner only Sun, Tue, Thu & Sat (subject to change).

Sottovento On the Beach $$$ *Ocean Point Residence, Hodges Bay, tel: 562 8330;* www.sottoventoantigua.com. Set in the Ocean Point complex, this restaurant uses seasonal local produce for its Italian and Mediter-ranean-influenced dishes. Main courses include their legendary bouil-labaisse and there's a range of interesting desserts. Reservations for dinner required. Daily breakfast, lunch and dinner.

EAST OF THE ISLAND

The Bay @ Nonsuch $$$ *Nonsuch Bay Resort, tel: 562 8000*; www.non suchbayresort.com. In a dramatic setting on a headland at Nonsuch Bay, diners are seated on terraces cascading down the hillside. The chef draws inspiration from around the world. Daily lunch and dinner.

Beach Bum Bar & Grill $ *Half Moon Bay, tel: 464 1974*. The ultimate beach bar delightfully situated on a pristine bay, serving probably the best Mahi wrap you're ever likely to eat. There is a huge choice of food and it's very reasonably priced. Daily 9am–5pm.

Mama's Fresh Homemade Pasta $ *Long Bay, tel: 562 7110*. A family-run beach café focusing on homemade Italian pastas, such as beef and spinach with cheese and tomato sauce, washed down with excellent rum punch. Shaded tables outside offer wonderful views over the beach and ocean. Cash only. Daily 9am–5pm (hours erratic).

ENGLISH HARBOUR AREA

Le Cap Horn $$$ *Dockyard Drive, English Harbour, tel: 460 1194*. French meets Italian: choose between refined French fare, where food is cooked on hot stones, or a very well-made pizza. Daily lunch and dinner, closed Thu.

Catherine's Café $$$ *Pigeon Point tel: 460 5050*; www.catherines-cafe. com. With new owners at the helm since 2017, it doesn't get much better than the French-inspired cuisine at this beach-chic restaurant over-looking the water; enjoy pan roasted mahi mahi then finish off with tarte tatin – to die for. Daily lunch and Wed–Fri dinner.

Cloggy's $$ *Antigua Yacht Club Marina, Falmouth Harbour, tel: 460 6910*. Dine outside on the wooden veranda for views of the yachts, or inside on comfy sofas. The menu is inspired by the owners' Dutch roots with a hint of Mediterranean influence. Wed–Sat lunch and dinner, Tue and Sun lunch only.

Copper and Lumber Store $$ *Nelson's Dockyard, tel: 460 1160*; www. copperandlumberhotel.com. Eat fine international cuisine inside this

wonderful stone hotel held together by huge wooden beams, or dockside in the lovely courtyard; grilled mahi mahi is a favourite. Renowned for its Seafood Fridays. Daily breakfast, lunch and dinner.

Incanto $$ *Antigua Slipway, English Harbour, tel: 789 4531;* www.incanto antigua.com. Sitting on a dock out over the water, Italian owner Rosella makes you feel right at home while whipping up truly delicious Italian dishes. After dinner chill out in the lounge bar on large sofas while watching the boats in front of you. Wed–Mon 11am–10pm.

Island Infusion $$ *Dockyard Drive, English Harbour, tel: 734 5671.* Set among the grounds of the Sailing Academy, grab a table by the water and prepare to enjoy local specials such as curried goat and jerked pork. Daily breakfast, lunch and dinner, closed Wed & Sun dinner.

Pillars Restaurant $$$ *Admiral's Inn, Nelson's Dockyard, tel: 460 1027;* www.admiralsantigua.com. Eat inside the 200-year-old inn or on the tree-shaded terrace looking out over the water. Seafood is a speciality with dishes like tuna tartare and grilled lobster *au gratin* receiving rave reviews. Daily breakfast, lunch and dinner.

Restaurant Downstairs $$$ *South Point, Yacht Club Drive, English Harbour, tel: 562 9600;* www.southpointantigua.com. Inspired by Asian, Mediterranean and Middle Eastern cuisine, this restaurant is the definition of island chic with a café-style vibe. The dining deck is suspended over the water. Daily 6–10pm.

Ristorante Paparazzi $$ *Dockyard Drive, English Harbour, tel: 720 3201.* Immediately on the water's edge, Paparazzi brings the home-style cooking of Italy to Antigua. Dishes are crammed with the freshest, quality ingredients and the wine list features fine wines from around the world. Tue–Sun 6–10.30pm.

Trappas $$ *Dockyard Drive, English Harbour, tel: 562 3534.* Small, vibrant and friendly bar and restaurant with an extensive international menu – anything from mackerel paté, sautéed mussels and homemade hummus to traditional West Indian curry. Reservations recommended. Daily 6–10pm.

WEST OF THE ISLAND

Carmichael's $$ *Sugar Ridge Hotel, Tottenham Park, tel: 484 3701*; www.sugarridgeantigua.com. Set in a stunning location high on the ridge, Caribbean cuisine meets the rest of the world – the chef's signature dishes include lobster medallion and Carmichael's boullibaisse. Reservations essential. Daily dinner only.

Castaways $$ *South Beach, Jolly Harbour, tel: 562 4446*; www.castawaysbeachclub.com. This established, quintessential beach restaurant is an island favourite serving local dishes with an Indian twist. There's always a party vibe and you can eat right on the sand. Breakfast, lunch and dinner.

Dennis Cocktail Bar and Restaurant $$ *Ffryes Beach, tel: 462 6740*. A classic Caribbean restaurant serving excellent local dishes; goat curry, fish stew, catch of the day, barbequed ribs and chicken are all on the menu. Dine or drink cocktails while watching a magical sunset. Tue–Sun from noon.

East $$$ *Carlisle Bay, Old Road, tel: 502 2855*; www.carlisle-bay.com/dining/east. In a wonderful cliffside setting, dinner at East offers a sophisticated experience and some of the best Asian food in Antigua. Carved Indonesian doors, dark wood and splashes of red set the scene for expertly created Japanese, Thai and Indonesian dishes. Daily 6.30–9.30pm.

Jacqui O's Beach House $$ *Sir Andy Roberts Drive, Crabbe Hill, Jolly Harbour, tel: 562 2218*. Definitely one for the 'in' crowd, so chill out and sample the fusion cooking at this popular beachfront restaurant. The menu changes often; highlights might include a rock fish bouillabaisse and a pineapple gazpacho, all carefully sourced locally. Tue–Sun 9am–8pm, closes at 5pm Tue and Wed.

Miracles $$ *Valley Road, Jolly Harbour, tel: 783 0045*; www.miraclessouthcoast.com. Here you'll find freshly caught fish every day – mahi mahi, snapper, wahoo, tuna and even shark. Try prawns cooked five different ways or pan-fried scallops. If you prefer meat, there is pork, goat and chicken. Daily 11am–1am.

The Nest $$ *Valley Church Beach, Jolly Harbour, tel: 562 7958*. Pretty little beach-front place that serves simple but well-prepared local food and great mixed drinks. The coconut shrimps come with a lovely dipping sauce and the conch fritters are to die for. A little hard to find down a dirt road with potholes but worth the trek if you're looking for something a bit quieter. Daily 11am–8pm (closing times erratic).

OJ's $$ *Crabbe Hill, tel: 460 0184*. There are great views over to Montserrat from this nautical-themed beach bar and restaurant, which serves some great seafood pasta, plus good fresh fish and barbequed ribs. Live music on some Friday and Sunday evenings. Daily 10am–9.30pm.

Sheer Rocks $$$ *Cocobay Resort, Valley Church, tel: 464 5283*; www.sheer-rocks.com. Imaginative dishes are served in a romantic setting; diners can enjoy their meal seated on small balconies with privacy provided by a sheer curtain. Tapas lunch is available. Day beds and plunge pool. Reservations recommended for dinner. Daily lunch, Mon–Sat dinner.

Turner's Beach Restaurant $$ *Turner's Beach, Johnsons Point, tel: 915 9429*. Popular with water-sports enthusiasts and families alike, Turner's offers a good-value menu. For everything from the fish cakes and conch fritters to red snapper and roti, it's well worth dropping by. Daily 10am–10pm.

BARBUDA

ArtCafé $$ *Two Foot Bay Road, Codrington, tel: 726 9118*; www.barbudaful.net. Primarily promoted as an art gallery, artist and owner Claire Frank is a wonderful cook, too. In lovely rustic surroundings, the food is fresh and interesting; venison red wine casserole with guava, shark kebabs and beautifully cooked barracuda, plus chicken, Johnny cakes and more. Must be pre-booked. Closed Sun.

Uncle Roddy's $ *Coral Group Bay, tel: 722 3050*. Located right on the beach, Barbuda's only totally solar-powered restaurant is run by the characterful Roddy. Although most famous for his barbequed lobster, he also serves grilled fish and chicken, all with rice and peas. Reservations required. Daily lunch and dinner.

A–Z TRAVEL TIPS

A SUMMARY OF PRACTICAL INFORMATION

A

ACCOMMODATION

A large proportion of visitors to Antigua stay in all-inclusive resorts. There is however a great diversity of accommodation for every budget, ranging from small hotels, beach clubs and guesthouses to independent villas, apartments and economical Caribbean-style houses. Unlike its neighbour, accommodation on Barbuda is limited and, at the time of writing, consists of two hotels, a guesthouse, cottages and a glamping site. The 2017 hurricane destroyed Barbuda's accommodation offering, including the longest established Coco Point Lodge, which is being rebuilt as Barbuda Ocean Club. A few establishments have reopened since and hopefully more will follow.

Off-season rates (April to December) can be as much as a third lower than those in the high season. Many hotels offer special rates, especially via the internet. A government tax of 12.5 percent is payable, plus a 10 percent service charge, but for all-inclusive package holidays this may already be included in the quote. Local tax rates are subject to change, so always check in advance.

For more details contact the Antigua Tourist Authority in London (tel: 020 7258 0070, www.antigua-barbuda.com). For information specifically on Barbuda see www.barbudaful.net. Other useful websites listing accommodation are www.antigua-barbuda.org, www.antiguahotels.org (Antigua Hotels and Tourist Association), www.antiguanice.com and www.airbnb.co.uk.

If you want to rent a villa, there are several websites dedicated to this, including www.caribrepvillas.com and www.antiguavillas.com.

AIRPORTS

V.C. Bird International Airport (ANU, tel: 484 2300; www.vcbia.com) lies approximately 4 miles (7km) northeast of St John's. No bus service operates at the airport but taxis are available. There are fixed rates from the airport to many destinations and hotels, which can be

obtained on arrival. For example a taxi from the airport to St John's is US$12, to English Harbour US$32 and Jolly Harbour US$25. Car rental companies are present at the airport (see Car hire).

A new, modern terminal building opened in early summer 2015 provides vastly improved facilities for passengers.

B

BICYCLES, QUADS AND SCOOTER HIRE

It is recommended that only experienced drivers should hire quad bikes or scooters, and helmets should always be worn. Scooter and quad-bike rentals are available from Chekes Rentals in English Harbour (tel: 723 9292; www.chekesrentals.com). Scooters are also available at Salty Dogs Rentals in Redcliffe Quay, St John's (tel: 562 8341; www.saltydogsrentals.com). Cycling is a good way to explore at a leisurely pace, but keep in mind the tropical heat and bumpy roads; always take plenty of water and use adequate sun protection. Bicycle rentals are available from Paradise Boat Sales in Jolly Harbour (tel: 562 7125; www.paradiseboats.com). On Barbuda check out Barbuda Rentals (tel: 721 9993; www.barbudarentals.com). Some hotels also rent out bikes. For more information on cycling see the Antigua Cycling Association (www.antiguacycling.com).

BUDGETING FOR YOUR TRIP

Many visitors to Antigua and Barbuda are on all-inclusive package holidays so most expenses incurred will usually be for tours or taxi rides. For those travelling independently, here are some average prices:

Flights: From the UK: from £600 return; from the US: $800 return

Accommodation: Rates for a double room in an average hotel or guesthouse around US$175 a night. Cheaper accommodation can be found but may not be on the beach.

Transport: A taxi tour costs around US$30 an hour for up to 4 pas-

sengers, plus a 10 percent tip. Buses are far cheaper but not always reliable.

Meals and drinks: An average three-course meal without drinks will cost around US$30 per person. A panini will be around US$14, a chicken salad US$13 and an ice cream US$6. A local beer US$2.50, lager US$3.50, glass of wine US$4, soft drink US$2, coffee US$4, English tea US$3.50, bottle of water US$2.

Sightseeing: The entrance fee to Nelson's Dockyard is US$8. Costs to some attractions are free or by donation, for example the National Museum of Antigua and Barbuda in St John's suggests US$3.

Tours: There are so many types of tours and prices will vary accordingly. A popular choice is to Stingray City, which costs around US$60. Antigua Rainforest Zip Line tours start at US$69. For more tours (see page 122).

C

CAR HIRE

The minimum age for hiring a car is determined by individual companies but is normally 21 years and all drivers must have held a licence for at least one year. A deposit may be made by credit card or by cash.

Among the most reliable agencies are:

Avis: Airport, tel: 462 2840; www.avis.com.

Dollar: Airport, tel: 462 0362; www.dollar.com.

Hertz: Carlisle Airport Road/ Heritage Quay/Airport, tel: 481 4440; www.hertz.com.

Budget: Airport, tel: 561 6399.

Thrifty: Carlisle Airport Road, tel: 462 9532; www.thrifty.com.

There are plenty of smaller companies, too, many of them located along the road running beside the airport. The Antigua Tourist Authority also has a list on their website (www.visitantiguabarbuda.com). Car hire starts from around US$45 a day.

During peak season (December to April) and especially in Antigua Sailing Week (late April) and Carnival (early August) be sure to book well in advance as cars can be hard to obtain.

CLIMATE

In reality, Antigua is a year-round destination, with little monthly difference in the amount of rainfall, temperature or cooling trade winds. Temperatures vary between 79°F (26°C) and 90°F (32°C), the warmest months tending to be July, August and September. The trade winds, a constant easterly sea breeze, are on tap to relieve the settling heat. The rainy season chiefly involves afternoon showers, euphemistically referred to as 'liquid sunshine', that come and go in a flash.

The hurricane season lasts from June to November, with the highest risk between mid-August and mid-October. Hurricanes are rare, but with an increase in hurricane damage in the past 30 years early warning systems are now in place.

		J	F	M	A	M	J	J	A	S	O	N	D
Max	°C	27	29	29	28	29	30	31	30	30	29	29	27
	°F	81	84	84	82	84	86	88	86	86	84	84	81
Min	°C	22	22	23	23	24	25	25	25	25	24	24	23
	°F	72	72	73	73	75	77	77	77	77	75	75	73

CLOTHING

Casual, cool and comfortable clothes are what you need. Antiguans are fairly conservative and may be offended at inappropriate dress; swimwear should be reserved for the beach. Don't wear bathing costumes or very short shorts when shopping or sightseeing in town, and stick to the recommended 'elegantly casual' dress in hotels and restaurants. Some venues are more formal than others and

may ask men to wear a jacket and tie. Winter evenings can be cool and a light wrap is occasionally welcome. For the most part rain showers are short and there is usually some form of shelter nearby.

CRIME AND SAFETY

Antigua and Barbuda are pretty safe places, with little violent crime. There is a certain amount of crime, as there is anywhere else in the world, and general precautions should be taken. Never leave valuables in a vehicle, even if it is locked. Don't take valuables to the beach, or leave items unattended. Don't purchase any illegal substances. Don't visit the more remote, isolated beaches by yourself. Avoid producing large amounts of cash in public, and be mindful of bags, pockets and cameras in busy places such as markets and at Carnival time. In the event of a crime call 999/911 or contact the local police (see also Police).

D

DISABLED TRAVELLERS

In general, facilities for disabled travellers on Antigua or Barbuda are not particularly apparent, although many resort hotels have accommodation suitable for visitors with disabilities, with specially adapted rooms. Wheelchair access may not be available in all resorts so check with the hotel on booking.

St John's: The town is mainly flat and most of the pavements have flat kerbs. There is disabled access to the shopping areas at Heritage and Redcliffe Quays, and there are accessible toilets located to the quay side of King's Casino. Local buses are not accessible for wheelchair users.

DRIVING

A temporary Antiguan licence, costing US$20/ EC$54, valid for three months, is required. They can be obtained on the spot from rental

companies and you must produce your national or international licence.

Hiring a car is the most convenient way to get around, but driving on the island can be a challenge. Large main roads are in relatively good condition but most others are bad, with many pot holes and decaying edges and few road markings. Beware, too, of goats that stray into the road. Street lighting is limited, and there are very few signposts. When there's a hurricane, road signs are the first thing to go and the last to be replaced. The government and the tourist office are well aware that this causes problems for visitors and there are plans for improvement, but no action so far. In some areas 'sleeping policemen' (speed bumps) can be very dangerous. The maximum speed limit throughout the island is 40mph but this is not generally enforced or regulated.

Some roads (especially to remote beaches) are only accessible by four-wheel-drive vehicles. Hitting a pot hole can cause an instant blow out, so always check for a spare tyre and parts to change a wheel before accepting the hire car. Parking is difficult in St John's and fines are imposed for illegal parking, but there are car parks at the bottom of High and Long streets and at the lower end of Church Street. Hire cars are denoted by R on the licence plate. Driving is on the left, as in the UK. Seat belts must be worn. You will need to call your car hire company in the event of a breakdown. There are several petrol stations in and around St. John's and scattered throughout the island.

E

ELECTRICITY

In Antigua and Barbuda the normal wattage is 110 volts, with sockets of the two flat-pin style and UK visitors will normally need travel plug adapters. However, many of the large resorts have UK-style sockets as well; check with your hotel beforehand.

EMBASSIES AND CONSULATES

UK: The British High Commission, Lower Collymore Rock, PO Box 676, Bridgetown, Barbados, tel: (246) 430 7800.

US: The Consular Agent, 2 Jasmine Court, Friars Hill Road, St John's, tel: 463 6531.

Canada: The Canadian High Commission, Bishop's Court Road, PO Box 404, Bridgetown, Barbados, tel: (246) 429 3550.

EMERGENCIES

Police/ambulance 911/999
Fire 462 0044
Air/Sea Rescue 562 1234
Police Headquarters 462 0125

G

GETTING THERE

By Air. There are frequent services to Antigua from the UK provided by Virgin Atlantic (www.virgin-atlantic.com), British Airways (www.britishairways.com) and Thomas Cook (www.thomascookairlines.com; only in winter).

From the US, American Airlines flies from New York (JFK) and Miami (www.aa.com), United (www.unitedairlines.com) from New York (Newark), and Delta (www.delta.com) from Atlanta several times a week; Air Canada (www.aircanada.com) has a regular service from Toronto, Canada.

There is no airport shuttle service but there is no shortage of taxis for independent travellers. Taxi companies at the Heritage Quay cruise ship dock include Evans Ellis Taxi Association (tel: 562 8181) and at the airport United Taxi Association (tel: 562 8259). The majority of people who arrive on all-inclusive holidays will be met by a pre-arranged taxi or minibus from their hotel.

Inter-island Travel. Antigua Barbuda Monserrat Air (ABM Air, tel: 562

7183, www.antigua-flights.com) operates scheduled flights and private charters between Antigua and Barbuda, and the island of Monserrat; daily flights but changes to schedules are made almost every day and often without notice; with a flight time of 18 minutes.

By Sea. Barbuda can be reached via the Barbuda Express (see page 131) ferry. Barbuda and the neighbouring islands can also be reached by catamaran on organised day-trips.

Most cruise ships dock at Heritage Quay or Nevis Street Pier and visitors typically have a day in port. Small boats and private yachts can anchor in St John's Harbour, English Harbour, Falmouth Harbour, Jolly Harbour.

GUIDES AND TOURS

Organised tours are a major part of holidaying on these islands, and it is advisable to take advantage of the numerous land and sea options available, from safari and eco-tours to boat charters and catamaran cruises. You can snorkel, kayak, sports fish, island hop, or zip through the air among the lush rainforest canopy. The sky is truly the limit.

Trips often include lunch and a visit to interesting sites on the islands (in the case of Barbuda this includes the Frigate Bird Sanctuary on Codrington Lagoon, see page 79, and most tours will pick up guests from their hotel.

A fun way to see the island is to take a taxi island tour. Most taxi drivers are qualified to show you the island and will be able to introduce you to aspects you would not easily be able to find on your own, such as local restaurants and hidden views. The tourist office in St John's or your hotel will be able to help you to choose your driver or preferred company.

A day trip to Barbuda or one of the other neighbouring islands – including Guadeloupe, Dominica, St Kitts and Nevis and Montserrat – is well worth making while you are in Antigua, and there are a number of ways to do this (see above). If you want to fly, Antigua's

V.C. Bird Airport is a central hub for LIAT airlines (www.liat.com) that organise flights to many of the islands. You can also arrange flights or boat trips through a tour operator or travel agent, many of whom have representatives at the major hotels. Reputable travel agents who arrange **island trips** include:

Bo Tours, tel: 462 6632; www.botours.net. One of the best operators for organising a special trip, with multilingual staff.

Caribbean Helicopters, tel: 460 5900; www.flychl.com. They offer trips to Montserrat, as well as 15- and 30-minute tours over Antigua.

Carib-World Travel, Woods Centre, tel: 480 2999; www.carib-world.com. Organises trips to Montserrat, as well as local tours on the island and catamaran cruises.

Jenny Tours, tel: 722 8188/9092; www.jennymontserrattours.com. Takes visitors by high-speed ferry and air to Montserrat and Barbuda.

The following are a small selection of the diverse specialised tours available:

Adventure Antigua, tel: 726 6355; www.adventureantigua.com. Try Eli's Eco Tour on a powercat – snorkelling, reef exploration and through the North Sound islands.

Antigua Nature Tours, Seatons, tel: 720 1761; www.antiguanaturetours.com. Kayaking, snorkelling in the North Sound Marine Park, and trips to Great Bird Island.

Antigua Paddles, Seatons, tel: 463 1944; www.antiguapaddles.com. An eco-adventure by kayak for all the family through mangroves, inlets and tiny islands.

Antigua V.I.P Tours, tel: 724 2129; www.antiguavipsafaritours.vpweb.com. Personalised, luxury land-based tours.

Catch the Cat, tel: 464 7113; www.catchthecatantigua.com/fishing.html. Deep sea and bottom fishing charters aboard *Mystic Amara II*.

Creole Antigua Tours, Jolly Harbour, tel: 770 4444; www.creoleantiguatours.com. Relax on a lobster lunch cruise.

Miguel's Holiday Adventure, tel: 772 3213; www.pricklypearisland. com. (Tue, Thu and Sat.) Has been operating charters to Prickly Pear Island for many years; lobster lunch is included in the price.

Ondeck, tel: 562 6696; www.ondecksailing.com. Based in Falmouth, try your hand at sailing while on a mini-cruise, or take part in an organised sailing course.

Reef Riders, tel: 728 5239; www.antiguareefriders.com. Follow the tour guide driving your own inflatable boat while exploring the west coast.

Salty Dogs Rentals, tel: 562 8341; www.saltydogsrentals.com. Climb aboard a jeep and follow your guide around the island, and off road.

South Coast Horizon, tel: 562 4074/5; www.southcoasthorizons.com. Offer a variety of eco-tours; kayaking among the mangroves and snorkelling on the reef.

Treasure Island Cruises, tel: 461 8675. Sail and snorkel, or circumnavigate the island.

Tropical Adventures, tel: 480 1225; www.tropicalad.com. Sleek catamarans take you round the island with a snorkelling stop or board a jeep for a land safari, or combine the two.

Wadadli Cats, tel: 462 4792; www.wadadlicats.com. Five catamarans at this long-standing operation offer three cruises: Great Bird Island, Cades Reef and a circumnavigation of the island.

268 Buggies, Jennings, tel: 788 5232; www.268buggies.com. Adrenaline-filled buggy tours off the beaten trail.

H

HEALTH AND MEDICAL CARE

There are no particular health problems to be aware of on the islands. No vaccinations are necessary by law but make sure you are up to date with tetanus, typhoid and hepatitis A. Check with your medical practitioner for any additional vaccinations that may be required. Bottled mineral water is widely available and visitors are often advised not to drink the tap water. Many drinks are full of

crushed ice and, if you want to take a chance, iced drinks and frozen cocktails don't seem to do any harm. However, if you are nervous ask for your drinks without ice.

Apart from minor stomach upsets, sunburn and heatstroke are the two most commonly experienced problems, and most can be avoided by using common sense. The Caribbean sun is very fierce, even when there are clouds in the sky, so be sure to take sensible precautions – wear a hat to protect your head and provide some shade, use a high-factor sunblock, stay out of the sun during the midday hours, and drink plenty of water. Aloe vera, a natural remedy, and other after-sun soothers are sold in pharmacies and hotel shops.

There is no malaria on the island but there is a risk from the Zika, Dengue and Chikungunya viruses, which are all spread by mosquito bites. Chik V, as it is known, is more prevalent after the rainy season. Dengue can be serious. Symptoms of the disease usually manifest from 3 to 14 days after infection and might include fever, headache, fatigue, a rash and nausea. The illness usually resolves and serious complications are uncommon but if symptoms worsen seek medical advice. Visitors are advised to take precautions to avoid bites by using insect repellent and appropriate clothing, by day as well as night.

All visitors should take out adequate insurance to cover medical costs (as well as loss or damage to property and an air ambulance to transport you home if necessary) before they leave home. Your travel agent will usually organise this for you when you make your booking.

Medical Care. There is one state-run hospital in Antigua, the Mount St John's Medical Centre at Michael's Mount (tel: 484 2700; www.msjmc.org). The standard of care is quite good.

The Adelin Medical Centre is on Fort Road, north of St John's (tel: 462 0866), and has some of the best facilities and doctors on the island.

The Hannah Thomas Hospital (formerly Spring View Hospital) in Codrington, Barbuda (tel: 460 0409) has a full-time resident doctor

and hosts visiting American doctors. The facility manages minor to moderate surgeries. Major medical emergencies are transferred to Antigua. The hospital was badly damaged by the 2017 hurricane and is awaiting rebuilding when funds become available.

If you should become ill while you are on holiday your hotel will arrange for you to see a doctor. For minor complaints, most of the large hotels have a duty nurse on the premises.

Pharmacies. There are numerous pharmacies on the island of Antigua, mostly in St John's. The majority open Mon–Sat 9am–5pm. Ceco Pharmacy on High Street is open daily 8.15am–midnight. Woods Pharmacy at the Woods Mall near St John's is the largest.

Dentists. There are many dentists on the island, although they can be hard to contact on public holidays and at weekends·

Dr SenGupta, Woods Mall, Friars' Hill Road, tel: 462 9312 (including out of hours emergencies).

Dr Bernard Evan-Wong, Gambles Medical Centre, Friars' Hill Road, tel: 462 3050.

Dr Jammula, Upstairs Nature's Family Store, Market Place, St John's, tel: 562 4972.

You can also ask your hotel for recommendations.

L

LANGUAGE

Although English is the only language ever adopted on the islands, you may wonder what Antiguans and Barbudians are saying when they chat in their lilting accents interspersed with African words. Everybody sooner or later acquires a few idiomatic phrases such as 'no big ting' or 'Antigua me come from'.

LGBTQ TRAVELLERS

Antiguan society is very macho and not tolerant of homosexuality, with certain laws in place. However, the pink dollar is accepted as

yet another facet of tourism, but overt public displays of affection are not recommended.

M

MEDIA

Newspapers. The *Observer* is Antigua's only daily publication. The Trinidad & Tobago *Guardian* and the Jamaican *Gleaner* are widely available. The *New York Times*, *USA Today* and a number of British newspapers are also available, mainly in hotel shops, but are usually a day old by the time they reach the islands.

Radio and television. There are several radio stations on the island, broadcasting a mixture of news, music and phone-in programmes: Observer Radio 91.1 FM; Liberty Radio ZDK 99 AM; ABS 90.3 FM; VYBZ 92.9 FM; Crusader Radio 107.5FM.

There is only one television station, Antigua and Barbuda Network (ABN), an internet-only service available via live streaming. Most hotels have satellite dishes with a variety of channels, mainly of North American origin.

MONEY

The currency used on both of the islands is the Eastern Caribbean dollar (currency code XCD, common usage EC$); one dollar is made up of 100 cents. The exchange rate is tied to the US dollar at approximately US$1 = EC$2.70. The coins (EC$1 and EC$2; 1, 2, 5, 10, 25 cents) look very much like English coins with the Queen's head on the front. US dollars are widely accepted in hotels, restaurants and shops, but you might be given your change in EC$ currency.

Major credit cards are also accepted in most hotels and restaurants, but always check in advance. Sterling can be exchanged in banks in St John's High Street, and at Woods Mall, Friars Hill Road, to the north of St John's.

US dollars are the best currency to take – either in cash or travel-

ler's cheques – although euros and sterling can be exchanged at banks but expect a poor rate. There are ATMs (cash machines) located outside several banks.

O

OPENING TIMES

Banks are usually open Mon–Thu 8am–1pm, 3pm–5pm, Fri 8am–noon, 3pm–5pm; some also open until noon on Saturday. Shops open Mon–Sat 8am–5pm (some close between noon and 1pm); many shops close at noon on Thursdays. Most government offices open Mon–Thu 8am–4.30pm, Fri 8am–3pm.

P

POST OFFICES

There are post offices at the bottom of Long Street, St John's (tel: 562 1929), Woods Mall, Nelson's Dockyard, All Saints Village and in Codrington, Barbuda. Postcards and letters can also be posted from your hotel. Post offices are generally open Mon–Fri 8.15am–noon, 1pm–3.30pm (Fri until 4pm), Sat 9am–noon.

Fedex – the agent in Antigua is Francis Trading on High Street, St John's (tel: 462 3339).

POLICE

Law enforcement in Antigua and Barbuda is carried out primarily by the Royal Police Force of Antigua and Barbuda. Police Headquarters are located in American Road in St John's (tel: 462 0125) with a second station in Newgate Street.

PUBLIC HOLIDAYS

1 January New Year's Day
1 November Independence Day

9 December V.C. Bird Day (formerly National Heroes Day)
25 December Christmas Day
26 December Boxing Day
Moveable Dates:
Late March–early April Good Friday, Easter Monday
First Monday in May Labour Day
Late May–early June Whit Monday
First Monday and Tuesday in August Carnival

T

TELEPHONE

To phone Antigua from the UK, dial 001 then the country/area code which is 268. For outgoing calls to the UK and the rest of Europe dial 011; for Canada, the USA and other Caribbean islands, dial 1; then add the country code (44 for the UK) and national phone number, omitting the first digit of the area code. For the Operator dial 0.

Phone cards for local and international calls can be purchased at hotels and some shops, with signs outside. There are coin and card phone boxes all over the island. As anywhere in the world, calls made from a hotel room are more expensive than those made from public phones.

Mobile phones. Many British and US mobile phones will work in Antigua and Barbuda, but check charges before leaving home. It is possible to buy or rent a mobile phone or you may purchase a SIM card locally on arrival in Antigua at the cost of around US$8 or EC$22, but your phone will have to be unlocked. You will be assigned a seven-digit phone number, which will remain yours. Local operators are Digicel (www.digicelantiguaandbarbuda.com) and Flow (www.discoverflow.co/antigua), both of which have the latest 4G coverage.

Internet. Hotels, private villas and apartments have internet access, but will often charge. There are cafés in St John's and English Harbour with internet access.

TIME ZONES

Antigua-Barbuda is on Atlantic Time, which is four hours behind Greenwich Mean Time (GMT) in (British) winter, and five hours behind in summer.

TIPPING

A 10–15 percent tip is the usual amount to give to taxi drivers, restaurants or the person who cleans your room. Restaurants may add a 10 percent service charge to the bill, so you don't need to tip on top of that, unless you feel it is deserved.

TOURIST INFORMATION

Antigua: Antigua and Barbuda Department of Tourism, Government Complex, Queen Elizabeth Highway, St John's, Antigua, West Indies, tel: 462 0480; email: deptourism@antigua.gov.ag, www.visitantigua barbuda.com.

Antigua and Barbuda Tourism Authority, 3rd floor, ACB Financial Centre, High Street, St. John's, Antigua, West Indies; tel: 562 7600; email: email: info@visitaandb.com, www.antigua-barbuda.org, open Mon–Fri 8.30am–4pm, Sat 8.30am–noon.

Antigua Hotels and Tourist Association, Island House, New Gates Street, PO Box 454, St John's, Antigua, West Indies; tel: 462 0374; www.antiguahotels.org.

Tourist Offices Abroad (see also www.visitantiguabarbuda.com):

Canada: Antigua and Barbuda Department of Tourism & Trade, 60 St Claire Avenue East, Suite 601, Toronto, Ontario, M4T 1N5; tel: 416 961 3085; email: info@visitaandb.com.

UK: Antigua and Barbuda Tourism Authority, 2nd Floor, 45 Crawford Place, London W1H 4LP; tel: 020 3668 3800; email: info@visitaandb.com.

US: Antigua and Barbuda Tourist Office, 3 Dag Hammarskjold Plaza, 305 E. 47th Street 6A, New York, NY 10017; tel: 212 541 4117/888 268 4227; email: info@visitaandb.com.

Embassy of Antigua and Barbuda, 3216 New Mexico Avenue, NW Washington, DC 20016; tel: 202 362 5122; email: embantbar@aol. com

TRANSPORT

By bus: Buses leave from St John's and they primarily serve the locals. The West Bus Station on Market Street, opposite the food market, and the East Bus Station on Independence Avenue, near the Cenotaph, are both easy to find. The west station serves the south and west, the east station the north and east of the island. There is no set timetable – buses leave when they are full. There are frequent departures during the week, fewer at weekends, with a frequent service between St John's and English Harbour. Route destinations are displayed but it is best to confirm with the driver. It is a slow method of transport but a good way to get the feel of island life and is very economical. Exact fares must be paid in EC$ coins. For further information of routes and fares visit www.bussto-panu.com.

By taxi: Taxis are recognisable by TX on the licence plate. Hotels will arrange reputable taxis for you and there are always a number of them hanging out around major tourist sights. Fares are not metered, but they are set by the government. Confirm the fare in advance and make sure of the currency you are quoted in (US$ or EC$). Hotels and the Antigua Tourist Office can provide information of taxi fares to the major points on the island. Fares are also posted at the airport.

If you are travelling to a remote area it is best to arrange a return trip. Drivers are given tourist information courses and should be informative about the island; a 10–15 percent tip is normal.

By ferry: The Barbuda Express (tel: 560 7989; www.barbudaex press.com) runs a once a day service between Antigua and Barbuda (two crossings Wed and Thu; round trip adult US$85). The crossing time is nominally advertised as 90 minutes but can take longer.

V

VISAS AND ENTRY REQUIREMENTS

Visitors to Antigua and Barbuda must have onward or return airline tickets and a passport valid for at least six months. Visitors are granted a maximum six months' stay. You should also be able to confirm your accommodation on the islands and you have enough money for your stay. It is a good idea to keep photocopies of essential documents and spare passport-sized photographs.

Nationals of the UK, EU, USA, Canada, Australia, New Zealand, Japan and the other Caribbean islands do not require a visa. Other visitors should check with their nearest Antigua consulate or Tourism Board before making the trip.

W

WEBSITES

Here are a few sites to help you plan your trip. Others can be found in the contact details for individual attractions, hotels and restaurants in this guide:

www.visitantiguabarbuda.com official site of the Antigua and Barbuda Department of Tourism

www.antigua-barbuda.org official site of the Antigua and Barbuda Tourism Authority

www.barbudaful.net comprehensive site on Barbuda

www.antiguanice.com general tourism site and accommodation

www.tiguideantigua.com Treasure Islands Guide, a comprehensive handbook published in Antigua

www.nationalparksantigua.com dedicated to the management of Antiguan National Parks

www.antiguaobserver.com for latest news of Antigua and Barbuda

www.gov.uk/foreign-travel-advice/antigua-and-barbuda British Government health and safety information

www.eagantigua.org the Environment Group of Antigua
www.antiguahistory.net/Museum/fauna.htm Antigua's flora and
fauna
www.windiescricket.com home of the West Indies Cricket Board

WEDDINGS

It is easy to get married in Antigua. Couples must visit the Ministry
of Legal Affairs at the Government Complex on Parliament Drive, St.
John's, with the following original documentation: valid passport; if
relevant, divorce decree; in the case of a widow/widower the marriage and death certificates. Both parties must be over 15. If under
18 written authorisation from parents or guardians is required.
There will be an informal interview, and the special licence will be
issued (fee US$150).

The next step is to visit the Registrar General's Office (tel: 462
0609, Mon–Thu 8.30am–4.30pm, Fri until 3pm), also on Parliament Drive, where other fees are payable: registering at the Court
House US$40; marriage certificate US$10; if the wedding is to be
performed outside the Court House, a Marriage Officer fee US$100.
The marriage must be solemnised in the presence of two or more
witnesses.

RECOMMENDED HOTELS

On Antigua, the largest development of accommodation spreads out from St John's, along the coast to the west and also to the north, where most of the best beaches are located. Not many visitors choose to stay in St John's itself, unless they are there for cricket or business. Another cluster of hotels and guesthouses has sprung up around English Harbour in the southeast, standing in idyllic spots with views over the harbour. There are also self-catering apartments and villas available to rent but as supermarkets are limited locally, you would need to go into St John's for shopping. At the time of writing (2019), there are only two hotels on Barbuda, so accommodation is limited to the very exclusive or fairly basic.

The selection below is listed alphabetically by region. As a basic guide, the price categories quoted are for a double room per night in high season (Dec–Apr), unless indicated as all inclusive (AI). For more information see Accommodation page 115.

$$$$$	over 750
$$$$	US$550–750
$$$	US$350–550
$$	US$150–350
$	below US$150

ST JOHN'S

Anchorage Inn $ *Anchorage Road, tel: 462 4065*; www.antiguaanchorage inn.com. Located between the town and the north coast, this family-owned 40-room inn is decorated in traditional Caribbean-style. Room options include studio apartments with kitchenette and private veranda overlooking the pool.

City View $ *Newgate Street, tel: 562 0259*; www.cityviewantigua.com. On the edge of town, this 50-room hotel is convenient for business people

with its modern conference facilities. Tastefully decorated rooms have air conditioning and a private patio; restaurant on site.

THE NORTH COAST

Antigua Village Beach Resort $$ *Dickenson Bay, tel: 462 2930*; www.antiguavillage.com. Nestled in a tropical garden, the 94 spacious studios, villas and suites are fully equipped for self-catering. There is a small grocery store and a freshwater swimming pool on site. The resort is sandwiched between two good restaurants.

Blue Waters Resort $$$$ *Soldier's Bay, tel: 462 0290*; www.bluewaters.net. Pure luxury on a serene sandy cove, with three restaurants, nightly entertainment, water sports, floodlit tennis court, seven freshwater pools, spa and a gym. Beautiful, spacious rooms and suites have fine views over the ocean and tropical gardens.

Buccaneer Beach Club $$ *Dickenson Bay, tel: 562 6785*; www.buccaneerbeach.com. Small and friendly Caribbean-style resort perfect for families, it offers one and two-bedroom villas with kitchen facilities and balconies or verandas. On-site amenities include a pool and laundry. Restaurants and supermarkets are within walking distance.

Dutchmans Bay Cottages $ *Dutchmans Bay, tel: 464 0207*; www.dutchmansbay.com. These seven Caribbean-style units lie right on the beach. Each authentic cottage is spacious, clean and self-contained with a fully-equipped kitchen, veranda and attractive furnishings.

Hodges Bay Resort & Spa $$$$ *Sandy Lane, Hodges Bay, tel: 625 3218*; www.eleganthotels.com/hodges-bay. Opened December 2018, the low-rise rooms here are state-of-the-art. Dip into an infinity pool, relax on the white-sand beach, indulge in the spa, or enjoy the extensive sporting facilities. There are three innovative dining options.

Le Jardin Creole $ *Hodges Bay, tel: 561 1835*. Cosy garden inn, run by charming hospitable hosts, where cottages and rooms are evocatively

named, such as Banana Cottage, Frangipani Room and Flamboyant Treehouse; small lagoon pool.

Jumby Bay Island $$$$$ *Al Jumbo Bay Island, tel: 462 6000*; www.oet kercollection.com/hotels/jumby-bay-island. Only reachable by boat, this luxurious hideaway is encircled by white-powdered beaches. Spread out across the island, the standard elegant and stylish rooms are in octagonal-shaped cottages with wrap-around terraces. Amenities include an oceanfront infinity pool, spa, water sports, tennis, and a selection of restaurants.

Ocean Point Resort & Spa $$ *Al Hodges Bay*, tel: 562 8330; www. oceanpointantigua.com; A Mediterranean-style resort with a large swimming pool, a massage centre on the beach and an Italian inspired restaurant. The bedrooms are bright and cheerful with balcony or veranda.

Sandals Grande Antigua $$$$ *Al Dickenson Bay, tel: 484 0100*; www. sandals.com. Tropical paradise meets European grandeur at this chic all-inclusive, couples-only resort. Choose between the Mediterranean Village and the Caribbean Grove, which between them offer 11 speciality restaurants, 6 pools and lots more. Popular for weddings.

Siboney Beach Club $$ *Dickenson Bay, tel: 462 0806*; www.siboney beachantigua.com. Almost hidden by palms and bougainvillea, the small and intimate Siboney has 12 suites in a three-storey building with a pool. Excellent food is served in the Coconut Grove restaurant. Request one of the top-floor balcony suites.

Starfish Halcyon Cove $$ *Al Dickenson Bay, tel: 462 0256*; www.rexre sorts.com/halcyon-cove. All-inclusive-only resort directly on a fabulous beach, with two restaurants (the Warri Pier extends over the sea), pool and tennis courts and water sports.

Trade Winds Hotel $$ *Dickenson Bay, tel: 462 1233*; www.twhantigua. com. Perched on a hilltop in lush gardens, with spectacular views over Dickenson Bay, this small and friendly hotel is a well-kept secret. Air-

conditioned rooms and suites have a fresh tropical feel, and the restaurant has sunset views.

EAST OF THE ISLAND

Blue Bay $ *Seatons, tel: 785 2877*; www.bluebayantigua.com. On top of a hill framed by lush gardens, this quiet serene bed and breakfast offers an authentic Caribbean stay in either a villa, suites or double room. Host Cecilia's moto is 'come as a guest leave as a friend', and her homemade food is a highlight.

Nonsuch Bay Resort $$$ AI *Nonsuch Bay, tel: 562 8000*; www.nonsuch bayresort.com. Carved out on a point on the southeast corner of the island, this resort opened in 2010. It offers 31 very spacious apartments, villas and cottages perched on the hillside. Top end open-air restaurant with stunning views.

Pineapple Beach Club $$$ AI *Long Bay, tel: 463 2006*; www.pineapple beachclub.com. Colourful beachfront property set in 25 acres (10 hectares) of cascading greenery. The open lobby is filled with hand-carved plantation furniture. Stylishly refurbished, some of the classically Caribbean rooms are located directly on the beach. There are five dining options, plus all the other facilities you would expect from an all-inclusive resort.

Verandah Resort & Spa $$$$ AI *Dian Bay, tel: 562 6845*; www.veran dahresortandspa.com. Bordering Devil's Bridge National Park, this eco-friendly resort encompasses two beaches, tropical landscape and villa-style suites decorated in Caribbean style. Extensive facilities include four restaurants, and a large free-form swimming pool.

ENGLISH HARBOUR AREA

Admiral's Inn $$ *Nelson's Dockyard, tel: 460 1027*; www.admiralsantigua. com. Set in four handsome 18th-century buildings in the heart of Nelson's Dockyard, with 23 individual rooms and suites. Pillars restaurant has a pretty and shady terrace while poolside Boom is housed in the for-

mer gunpowder house. A free boat shuttle transports guests to a small beach in the outer harbour.

Antigua Yacht Club Marina Resort $$ *Falmouth Harbour, tel: 562 3030; www.aycmarinaresort.com/resort.* The resort comprises 30 suites/studios with kitchenettes and a 19-room hotel, both decked out with wooden Indonesian furniture. Guest rooms offer vistas of either Falmouth Harbour or the tropical gardens. There are plenty of restaurants nearby.

Catamaran Hotel $$ *Falmouth Harbour, tel: 460 1036; www.catama ranantigua.com.* With just 14 rooms and suites, each with an ocean view and full kitchen facilities, this friendly hotel sits on the water's edge with views of Falmouth Harbour.

Copper and Lumber Store Historic Inn $$$ *Nelson's Dockyard, tel: 460 1160; www.copperandlumberstore.com.* This fine example of Georgian architecture houses 14 suites and studios in a meticulously reconstructed warehouse. The decor is in keeping with the period and rooms are named after Admiral Nelson's ships.

The Inn at English Harbour $$$$ *Nelson's Dockyard, tel: 460 1014; www. theinnantigua.com.* The perfect balance of a Colonial-style with boutique luxury, this exclusive hotel has just 28 rooms and stands on a secluded sleepy bay – the perfect honeymoon retreat. Facilities include two restaurants and a spa.

Ocean Inn $$ *English Harbour, tel: 463 7950; www.theoceaninn.com.* Small good-value hotel on a hillside overlooking the harbour; choose from budget rooms with shared bathroom to villas with stunning views. A pretty garden encloses the small pool; 10 minutes' walk from restaurants and bars.

South Point $$$$ *Yacht Club Drive, English Harbour, tel: 562 9600; www. southpointantigua.com.* Opened in 2014, the sleek, contemporary open-plan suites at South Point enjoy front row views of the marina. State-of-the-art facilities, including a pool and waterfront restaurant, attract a cosmopolitan crowd.

St James's Club $$$$ *Al Mamora Bay, tel: 460 5000*; www.stjames clubantigua.com. Situated on a 100-acre (40-hectare) peninsula, St James's benefits from two magnificent beaches – one on the Atlantic Ocean the other on the calm Caribbean waters. The variety of low-rise, stylish accommodation is concealed among lush green grounds with a marina, five restaurants, six pools, tennis, spa, and water sports.

Villa Touloulou $$$ *English Harbour, tel: 561 6395*; www.villatouloulou. com. Perched amid lush green gardens on the hillside, with views over the yacht-filled bay, three air-conditioned studios and apartments are individually appointed to a high standard. The many restaurants in English Harbour are within walking distance.

WEST OF THE ISLAND

Carlisle Bay Resort $$$$ *Old Road, tel: 502 2855*; www.carlisle-bay. com; Located on a spectacular beach in an unspoiled setting with expansive bay and tropical wooded views. The plantation style of the spacious rooms reflects a chic, cool edginess. On-site facilities include four restaurants – many facing onto the beach – a spa, tennis courts, water sports centre, library and movie screening room.

Cocobay Resort $$$ *Al Ffryes Beach, tel: 562 2400*; www.cocobayresort. com. Crowning a hilltop, this collection of pastel cottages and authentic plantation houses – decked out in custom-designed wooden furniture with hammocks on the balcony – is a real Caribbean experience.

Cocos Hotel $$$$ *Al Valley Church, tel: 562 3444*; www.cocoshotel.com. These 34 traditional cottages, complete with gingerbread fretwork and personal hammock, are built on a bluff overlooking Jolly Harbour beach. Cocos Restaurant is in a romantic setting overlooking the bay; swimming pool and bar.

Curtain Bluff $$$$$ *Al Morris Bay, tel: 462 8400*; www.curtainbluff.com. Sitting on a dramatic promontory, flanked by lovely beaches on both sides, this is one of the island's most amazing resorts. Curtain Bluff accepts just 146 guests, at most, in 72 rooms and (mostly) suites, all with

staggering views. Peerless service enhances exceptional facilities, and first-class dining. Closed mid-Aug–late Oct.

Galley Bay Resort & Spa $$$$ *Al Galley Bay, tel: 462 0302*; www.galleybayresort.com. Adult only, inclusive resort on the edge of a lagoon and bird sanctuary. Most of the 98 tastefully decorated rooms and Gauguin cottages are tucked into the tropical landscape along the pristine beachfront. Guests benefit from four restaurants.

Hawksbill by Rex Resorts $$ *Al Five Islands Village, tel: 462 0301*; www.rexresorts.com/antigua/hawksbill. Adults only resort set on an impressive 37-acre (15-hectare) site, with four private, white sand beaches. Housed in low-rise buildings, the wide range of accommodation options is all nestled among the palms.

Hermitage Bay $$$$$ *Al Five Islands Village, tel: 562 5500*; www.hermitagebay.com. In total harmony with its peaceful and secluded setting, 30 individual hillside suites are decorated in contemporary colonial style and some have private plunge pools with decking. Enjoy an ocean-side restaurant and bar, infinity-edge pool, hillside spa, and impeccable service.

Keyonna Beach Resort $$$ *Al Turners Beach, tel: 562 8880*; www.keyonnabeachresortantigua.com. Small-scale couples-only resort in a beach front location. Guest rooms take the form of quaint chalets, some with a private plunge pool. The restaurant features a multi-tiered wooden terrace offering great views.

Starfish Jolly Beach Resort $$$ *Al Jolly Beach, tel: 462 0061*; www.starfishresorts.com/resort/starfish-jolly-beach-resort. This large family resort (464 rooms), with a highly organised activities schedule, sits on what is said to be one of Antigua's best beaches. The various room rates available will suit every budget. Extensive facilities include two pools, five restaurants, spa, and kids' club.

Sugar Ridge $$$$ *St Mary's, tel: 562 7700*; www.sugarridgeantigua.com. Sugar Ridge is a fine boutique hotel that, with its elevated position, cap-

tures panoramic views of superb palm-lined beaches. Facilities include 60 deluxe rooms (some with plunge pools), three swimming pools, spa, gym, and Carmichael's fine- dining restaurant.

Villas at Sunset Lane $$ *Sunset Lane, McKinnons, tel: 562 7791*; www.villa satsunsetlane.com. Nestled on a hillside, this 10-room vibrant pink hotel (adults only) is just a 5-minute stroll from the sands at Dickenson Bay. There is a nice central pool and breathtaking views of the sea from the balcony.

BARBUDA

Art Café $ *tel: 726 9118*; www.barbudaful.net. Just outside Codrington village, on the road to Two Foot Bay, artist Claire Frank welcomes guests into her lovely home with one large double bedroom for rent. Perfect for independent travellers wanting to experience island life. A small café (Claire is a great cook) and art gallery are also on site and she will organise tours.

Barbuda Belle Hotel $$ *Cedar Tree Point, tel: 783 4779*; www.barbuda belle.com. Forced to close after hurricane Irma, the rebuilt Barbuda Belle opened its doors again in 2018 with new additions: a second restaurant and spa. Family owned, the hotel features eight bungalows set on a remote pink-sand beach, each rustic yet plush in style with a large balcony and stunning views. Solar powered, the hotel combines comfortable luxury and environmental sustainability. Closed Aug–Nov.

Barbuda Cottages $$ *tel: 722 3050*; www.barbudacottages.com. Standing on the southwest coast, these two self-contained, eco-friendly cottages (one and three bed) are directly on a fabulous stretch of beach and offer front-row seats of possibly the best sunsets ever. Closed Aug–Nov.

Frangipani Glamping $ *tel: 788 2134*; www.barbudaful.net. This eco-glamping site on the northeast coast, owned by two local sisters, offers a wooden Cabana with a large bed and outdoor kitchen and bathroom. The stunning beach is just over the sand dunes. Reconnect with nature, catch and cook your own lobster and enjoy the chance to get away from it all. There are plans to build a guesthouse next door.

INDEX

PLAN & BOOK
YOUR TAILOR-MADE TRIP

BRAZIL

CHILE

ECUADOR

TAILOR-MADE TRIPS & UNIQUE EXPERIENCES CREATED BY LOCAL TRAVEL EXPERTS AT INSIGHTGUIDES.COM/HOLIDAYS

Insight Guides has been inspiring travellers with high-quality travel content for over 45 years. As well as our popular guidebooks, we now offer the opportunity to book tailor-made private trips completely personalised to your needs and interests. By connecting with one of our local experts, you will directly benefit from their expertise and local know-how, helping you create memories that will last a lifetime.

HOW INSIGHTGUIDES.COM/HOLIDAYS WORKS

STEP 1

Pick your dream destination and submit an enquiry, or modify an existing itinerary if you prefer.

STEP 2

Fill in a short form, sharing details of your travel plans and preferences with a local expert.

STEP 3

Your local expert will create your personalised itinerary, which you can amend until you are completely satisfied.

STEP 4

Book securely online. Pack your bags and enjoy your holiday! Your local expert will be available to answer questions during your trip.

INSIGHT  GUIDES

ANTIGUA
& BARBUDA
POCKET GUIDE